The
Pomeranian

An Owner's Guide To

A HAPPY HEALTHY PET

Howell Book House

Howell Book House
A Simon & Schuster Macmillan Company
1633 Broadway
New York, NY 10019

Library of Congress Cataloging-in-Publication Data
Jones, Happeth.
The pomeranian : an owner's guide to a happy, healthy pet / Happeth Jones
    p cm.
ISBN: 0-87605-479-3
1. Pomeranian dogs. I. Title
SF429.P8J64 1996
636.7'6—dc20   96-193
              CIP
Manufactured in the United States of America
10 9 8 7 6 5 4 3 2 1

Series Director: Dominique De Vito
Series Assistant Directors: Ariel Cannon, Sarah Storey
Book Design: Michele Laseau
Cover Design: Iris Jeromnimon
Illustration: Jeff Yesh
Photography:
    Front and back cover Photos by Paulette Braun/Pets by Paulette
    Courtesy American Kennel Club: 17, 18
    Marcia Adams: 57
    Joan Balzarini: 96
    Mary Bloom: 23, 96, 136, 145
    Paulette Braun/Pets by Paulette: 8, 11, 12, 16, 20, 27, 34–36, 39, 47, 64, 58, 93
    Buckinghamhill American Cocker Spaniels: 148
    Sian Cox: 134
    Dr. Ian Dunbar: 98, 101, 103, 111, 116–117, 122–123, 127
    Happeth Jones: 14, 28, 53
    Dan Lyons: 96
    Cathy Merrithew: 129
    Julie Moreno: 45
    Liz Palika: 133
    Cheryl Primeau: 2–3, 7, 26, 29, 30, 37, 40, 42, 51, 85
    Janice Raines: 132
    Sarah Storey: 54–56
    Judith Strom: 22, 43, 96, 107, 110, 128, 130, 135, 137, 139–140, 144, 149–150
    Toni Tucker: 5
    Kerrin Winter & Dale Churchill: 96–97
    Zuma Press: 24, 61, 71
Production Team: Trudy Brown, Jama Carter, Kathleen Caulfield, Trudy Coler,
    Amy DeAngelis, Pete Fornatale, Matt Hannafin, Vic Peterson, Terri Sheehan
    and Marvin Van Tiem III.

Contents

Welcome
to the
World
of the

part one

Pomeranian

External Features of the Pomeranian

Skull

Stop

Muzzle

Crest

Neck

Shoulder

Back

Stifle or Knee

Toes

Hock

chapter 1

What
Is a
Pomeranian?

Ask Pomeranian owners the above question and most will answer: "The little dog who thinks it can." There he stands, all of five pounds, and thinks he's fifty-five. Breeders may have made the Pom's body smaller but they didn't reduce his self-image, and today's Pom thinks he's still a large dog. The elements that make up this little ball of fluff with the big personality involve his ancestry, which you can read about in Chapter 2; his personality, which Chapter 3 explores more fully; and the official "breed standard."

5

What Is the Standard and Why Do We Need It?

All purebred dogs are created artificially. When man discovered that he had more to eat because his floppy-eared, liver-and-white dog pointed at quail, he conscientiously bred to retain these traits. Selective breeding is how every purebred dog got its start, but breeders, being human, did not all agree on what traits to reproduce. Different owners would make parentage choices that had the potential to drastically change or hinder the development of the breed. For instance, in making the Pom smaller, breeders would mate small size to small size, but some considered fifteen pounds small and others, five pounds. Therefore, in order to create and preserve the breeds, the producers needed guidance as to what traits, structure and type to cultivate.

They acquired the needed guidance by forming organized breed clubs. Members of these clubs then compiled written descriptions, called breed standards, of the perfect representative of their breed. Early breeders used these standards as blueprints for their breeding programs, and with few revisions, they are still used today. Many local clubs represent a breed, but only the national breed club, called the parent club, decides standard revisions. In the United States, the American Pomeranian Club is the parent club that guards the breed ideal for the Pomeranian.

The breed standard depicts the perfect dog—a concept to work for—it doesn't mean something is wrong if your pet doesn't perfectly fit the ideal. Even top show dogs don't measure up to the model in every way. So if

---

WHAT IS A BREED STANDARD?

A breed standard—a detailed description of an individual breed—is meant to portray the *ideal* specimen of that breed. This includes ideal structure, temperament, gait, type—all aspects of the dog. Because the standard describes an ideal specimen, it isn't based on any particular dog. It is a concept against which judges compare actual dogs and breeders strive to produce dogs. At a dog show, the dog that wins is the one that comes closest, in the judge's opinion, to the standard for its breed. Breed standards are written by the breed parent clubs, the national organizations formed to oversee the well-being of the breed. They are voted on and approved by the members of the parent clubs.

---

your Suzie-Q has ears like a jackrabbit, and the Standard calls for tiny ears, don't get upset; she's as good as any other Pom, but to preserve breed type you wouldn't mate her to a dog that also sported jackrabbit ears. Remember, if breeders mated purebred dogs indiscriminately, breed types would disappear.

Studying the Standard

Since the Pomeranian is a companion dog, the standard ranks temperament and appearance high in importance. It also calls for soundness. As a smaller version of the Nordic dog, the Pomeranian, if enlarged, should be able to pull a sled and work in snow. The standard is in italics, and the author's comments follow.

The Pomeranian has an alert, intelligent expression.

I. GENERAL APPEARANCE   *The Pomeranian in build and appearance is a cobby, balanced and short-coupled dog. He exhibits great intelligence in expression and is alert in character and deportment.*

This section calls for a cobby, balanced dog, but it may leave you wondering what cobby means or how to define balance. A cobby dog is as long or shorter than he is tall; try to picture him as a circle in a square. A balanced Pomeranian fits together logically and in proportion. For instance, a small, delicately boned Pom with a large, coarse head looks unbalanced because his head type doesn't match his body type. A balanced Pom displays legs in proportion to his body: neither so short as to make him appear dumpy nor so long as to make him look like he is walking on stilts.

The general appearance segment also calls for an expression that imparts great intelligence. It tells us the Pom has an alert character and that he behaves accordingly. A stupid or dull Pom would not make a good comrade, so intelligence is an essential trait for this breed. His alertness not only makes him a superb watchdog, but adds to the "I'm special" attitude he exhibits.

The Pomeranian's thick coat reflects his Nordic ancestry.

II. SIZE, PROPORTION AND SUBSTANCE: Size

The weight of the Pomeranian for exhibition is from three to seven pounds. The ideal size for show specimens is four to five pounds.

Proportion *The Pomeranian in build and appearance is a cobby, balanced, short coupled dog. The legs are of medium length in proportion to a well balanced frame.*

Substance *The body is well ribbed and rounded. The brisket is fairly deep and not too wide.*

The standard calls for a dog that weighs from three to seven pounds. This broad weight range allows a dramatic difference in appearance to occur between a three-pounder and a seven-pounder. According to the standard both sizes are equal. The preferred weight of the Pom is in the middle of these two extremes—four to five pounds.

The proportions of the Pomeranian make his look fit the circle-in-a-square image. Measure the length of the dog from his shoulders to the root of the tail and the height from the shoulders to the ground. A dog with proper proportion is as long, or shorter, than he is tall.

His chest, called the brisket, goes deep enough to reach the elbow. His well-rounded body is not too wide, but has substance.

III. HEAD *Well proportioned to the body, wedge-shaped, with a fox-like expression.*

Eyes *Bright, dark in color, and medium in size, almond-shaped and not set too far apart nor too close together. Pigmentation around eye rims must be black, except self-colored in brown and blue.*

Ears *Small, carried erect and mounted high on the head placed not too far apart.*

Skull *Not domed in outline. A round, domey skull is a major fault.*

Muzzle *There is a pronounced stop with a rather fine but not snipy muzzle. Pigment around the lips must be black, except self-colored in brown and blue.*

Bite *The teeth meet in a scissors bite in which part of the inner surface of the upper teeth meet and engages part of the outer surface of the lower teeth. One tooth out of line does not mean an undershot or overshot mouth. An undershot mouth is a major fault.*

Nose *Pigment on the nose must be black, except self colored in brown and blue.*

The standard calls for a wedge-shaped head but does not define the width of the wedge. Keep in mind that a narrow wedge makes the head look like a Sheltie's and a wide wedge will give the Pom a Chow Chow appearance. The correct wedge falls in the middle range and helps keep the Pomeranian head from developing a dwarfing effect.

A side effect of breeding dogs down to a tiny size is the tendency for small dogs to take on dwarflike features, such as a flattened muzzle, bulging round eyes, domed heads, bowed legs and heavier bone. The developers of breeds like the Pug, Pekingese and Brussels Griffon used this tendency to their advantage. Some Poms display a sweet face, with round eyes, rounder skull and shortened muzzle, called a baby-doll face. Continued breeding of this admittedly precious look would eventually give the Pom a Pekingese face. The standard guides us away from this dwarfing effect by requiring a wedge-shaped, undomed head with a pronounced stop.

The standard calls for a foxlike expression, and the important word to remember here is "expression." The Pom does not look like a long-muzzled, big-eared fox, but exhibits the quick, alert, watchful expression of one. The **Bite, Eyes** and **Ears** sections read reasonably clearly. Recognize that the almond-shaped eyes and small high-set ears add to the fox-like expression.

IV. NECK, TOPLINE AND BODY: Neck   *The neck is rather short, its base set well back on the shoulders.*

Topline   *is level.*

Body   *The body is cobby, being well ribbed and rounded.*

Chest   *The brisket is fairly deep and not too wide.*

Tail   *The tail is a characteristic of the breed. It turns over the back and is carried flat, set high.*

The **Neck, Topline and Body** segment states that the Pomeranian's neck is set well back on the shoulders, which allows for that proud carriage of the head that shows his jaunty "I can" attitude. A Pom with a neck that is not set well back will carry his head forward as he walks. The proper set and carriage of the tail creates the essential look of the Pom. A tail set up high and flat on the back with the feathering touching the neck ruff pulls the appearance of the Pom into a circle. A low-set tail makes the Pom look long and gives him a rectangular appearance. Some tails curl, and while the standard doesn't address this, a tight curl takes away from the desired circle appearance. The curl may even cause the tail to lay to the side of the dog's body.

V. FOREQUARTERS: Shoulders *The Pomeranian is not straight in shoulder, but has sufficient layback of shoulders to carry the neck proudly and high.*

Forelegs *The forelegs are straight and parallel, of medium length in proportion to a well balanced frame.*

Pasterns *The Pomeranian stands well up on toes. Down in pasterns is a major fault.*

Dewclaws *Dewclaws on the forelegs may be removed.*

Feet *The Pomeranian stands well up on toes.*

VI. HINDQUARTERS: Angulation *Hindquarters and forequarters should be of equal angulation.*

Legs *The hocks are perpendicular to the ground, parallel to each other from hock to heel, and turning neither in nor out. Cow hocks or lack of soundness in hind legs or stifles is a major fault. Dewclaws, if any, on the hind legs are generally removed.*

The Standard is the blueprint by which dog show contestants are judged.

In the **Forequarter and Hindquarter** sections notice the emphasis on soundness in the Pomeranian's legs. Remember the Pom, if enlarged, should be like any other Nordic dog. Small size is not an excuse to accept bad stifles or lame legs. Today's Pom may not be a working dog, but he still needs strong healthy legs to run and play. After all, how can he be a lapdog unless his legs are hardy enough to allow him to jump on your lap? Straight parallel legs present efficient movement.

A Pom who stands well up on his toes has cat-shaped feet that almost disappear in his fur.

VII. COAT   *Coat type on head, legs and tail differs from body coat.*

Head coat   *Head coat is tightly packed and shorter in length than that of the body.*

Body coat   *Double coated; a short, soft, thick coat consisting of guard hairs, which must be harsh to the touch in order to give the proper texture for the coat to form a frill of profuse, stand-off, straight hair. A soft, flat or open coat is a major fault.*

Tail coat   *It is profusely covered with hair.*

Leg coat   *The front legs are well feathered and the hindquarters are clad with long hair or feathering from the top of the rump to the hocks.*

Trimming   *Trimming for neatness is permissible around the feet and up the back of the legs to the first joint; trimming of unruly hairs on the edges of the ears and around the anus is also permitted. Overtrimming (beyond the location and amount described in the breed Standard) should be heavily penalized.*

The **Coat** section reflects the Pom's Nordic ancestry, and of all the elements in the standard this is, other than size, the one that most defines his look. The harsh outer coat repels water and snow, and the dense undercoat keeps him warm. This type of coat does not lay flat, or split down the middle, but stands off from the body, giving the Pom his round majestic look. The proper coat tangles less and is easier to groom. The standard uses the word "harsh" to describe the texture of the guard hairs, but the outer coat doesn't really feel hard to the touch. The hairs feel tougher than the undercoat, but not as hard as a wire-haired coat.

VIII. COLOR: Classifications *The open classes at Specialty shows may be divided by color as follows: Open Red, Orange, Cream, Sable; Open Black, Brown and Blue; Open Any Other Allowed Color.*

Acceptable colors to be judged on an equal basis. Any solid color, any solid color with lighter or darker shadings of the same color, any solid color with sable or black shadings, parti- color, sable and black and tan. Black and tan is black with tan or rust, sharply defined, appearing above each eye and on the muzzle, throat and forechest, on all legs and feet and below the tail. Parti-color is white with any other color distrib- uted in even patches on the body and a white blaze on the head. A white chest, foot or leg on a whole-colored dog (except white) is a major fault.

Color The color section of the standard causes the most confusion to Pom owners. This breed comes in a variety of colors and shades and sometimes it is diffi- cult to know what a certain color, such as beaver, looks like, or whether or not a color fits the rules of the standard. In studying this section, let's start with the acceptable color definitions. Any solid color: Red, orange, black, blue, chocolate, cream, white, and beaver all fit this category.

Red Often dark oranges are mistakenly called red. A true red comes close to a rich Irish Setter color.

Orange A clear bright color, and currently the most popular of Pomeranian colors. Orange ranges from a deep rust through a rich gold to a blond shade. Breeders prefer the deep gold over the washed-out blond shade.

Black The glimmer of a rich blue-black sheen is more desirable than a coat dusted with a rusty tint.

Blue   A rather rare color today, blue is hard to describe. It is a slate grey color with more of a bluish tint than a grey one. A blue dog must have a blue nose.

Chocolate   This color looks like rich chocolate in hue; the dog's nose also must show the chocolate color.

Cream   The cream color flows evenly throughout the coat with no shades of white or yellow. Black-tipped hairs on the coat make the dog a cream sable.

The standard can be interpreted either for or against the brindle color.

White   A pure snow-white color with no shades of yellow behind the ears or on the coat. The nose and eye rims on a white dog must be black.

Beaver   A very rare color, beaver has been called everything from washed-out chocolate to beige. This color is sort of a pale, soft, greyish-beige, taupelike hue. The dog's nose should be the same shade.

Any solid color with lighter or darker shadings of the same color   Orange dogs darker on the back, with the color lighter under the tail and on the chest, fit in this category. So would a red with orange breeches, as orange is a dilution of red. Note that the color, though lighter, must be the same hue. An orange dog with white under the tail or chest is two colors and would be considered a mismark.

Any solid color with sable or black shadings   Any color, cream, orange, grey, etc., with black shadings. This includes a black mask, black saddle and black tips to the guard hairs. Some dogs may display a clear orange with only the back and the mask showing black, and some, called shaded sables, may have sabling throughout the coat.

Black and tan and parti-colors   This section reads reasonably clearly and doesn't need further elaboration, except to note that the color patches on a parti-color can be any color.

Brindle, chocolate and tan, blue and tan   These three colors may or may not be classified as acceptable colors as per the standard. It all depends on how you interpret it. Therefore, some judges penalize these colors and others award them the ribbon. Chocolate and tan could technically be defined as a solid color with lighter shadings, blue and tan could be defined as a diluted black and tan, and many claim the brindles are solid colors with black shadings. Others claim these colors don't belong because the standard doesn't clearly describe them. Whatever the viewpoint, the current standard does not disqualify any dog for deviation of color.

IX. GAIT   *The Pomeranian moves with a smooth, free but not loose action. He does not elbow out in front nor move excessively wide nor cow-hocked behind. He is sound in action.*

The Pom with a proper gait doesn't bounce up and down, lift his front legs with a bent knee or move with his legs real close together. He covers ground in a smooth action with front legs that reach out as far as his nose and hind legs that drive hard from the rear.

X. TEMPERAMENT   *He exhibits great intelligence in expression, and is alert in character and deportment.*

Brave, sweet and loving, the Pomeranian will dedicate himself to his owner; friendly, intelligent and classy, he is also a character; one who thinks he can.

THE AMERICAN KENNEL CLUB

Familiarly referred to as "the AKC," the American Kennel Club is a nonprofit organization devoted to the advancement of pure-bred dogs. The AKC maintains a registry of recognized breeds and adopts and enforces rules for dog events including shows, obedience trials, field trials, hunting tests, lure coursing, herding, earthdog trials, agility and the Canine Good Citizen program. It is a club of clubs, established in 1884 and composed, today, of over 500 autonomous dog clubs throughout the United States. Each club is represented by a delegate; the delegates make up the legislative body of the AKC, voting on rules and electing directors. The American Kennel Club maintains the Stud Book, the record of every dog ever registered with the AKC, and publishes a variety of materials on purebred dogs, including a monthly magazine, books and numerous educational pamphlets. For more information, contact the AKC at the address listed in Chapter 13, "Resources," and look for the names of their publications in Chapter 12, "Recommended Reading."

chapter 2

The Pomeranian's Ancestry

Casey struts over to the chain-link fence that encloses his pen. With an arrogant tilt to his head he looks out at the surrounding yard. His eyes scan to the right side of the lawn, then flick to the left. The grass, finally clear of the intruding squirrel, lays green and peaceful. Casey stiffens his rear legs, digs in his toes and flinging his legs back and forth tosses dirt in the air. Then, grunting little indignant huffs, he swaggers past the fence. Satisfied that all's well in his domain, he trots to the ramp that leads to his doggie door.

He runs up the ramp, sits down on the platform in front of the door and surveys his realm. His hair, with its majestic ruff framing his face, puffs around him like a royal mantle. He rests there, looking out with a regal expression in his eyes. Anyone passing by would realize at a glance that he is a "Little King."

Casey accepts this title as his due; after all, he is a Pomeranian, and his breed's long association with the sovereign classes, combined with its ancient blood-lines, support his view that he is, indeed, a royal dog.

Early History

The Pomeranian goes far back in history. Over 10,000 years ago a Spitz type of dog, the first of the Nordic group, made its appearance. These northern forest dogs, believed to be the first type of dog associated with man, include the Akita, Malamute, Norwegian Elkhound, Samoyed, Keeshond, Chow Chow, Finnish Spitz, Schipperke and Pomeranian.

Ch. Golden Twinkle of Floraland looks every bit the royal dog.

Curled tails, except for the Schipperke, erect ears, dense undercoats, and harsh outer coats characterize the Nordic group. Members of this group closely resemble each other and the Pom looks like a smaller version of a Keeshond, Elkhound or Samoyed.

The earlier Pomeranians differed in appearance from our current tiny version; they weighed between thirty and thirty-five pounds, with larger ears, longer muzzles and longer backs. They didn't have the wide variety of colors of our present-day Pom. White or biscuit seemed to be the most common color, with some black, blue, and brown dogs. Some breed historians theorize that a yellow-coated dog preceded the white one. Early literature doesn't usually mention the parti-color, but some paintings in the 1790s show Poms with this pattern, so it did exist.

The Pomeranian started with a commonplace back-ground. Along with the rest of the Nordic group he herded animals and pulled sleds, but even during the plebeian years of his history he managed to associ-ate with the elite. Greek pottery portrays the Pom romping with Apollo and Aphrodite, and drawings of him appear in Egyptian tombs. Tombs, I might add, made for Egyptian kings. Sometime before 1872, the Pom left his working background to join dogdom's leisure classes and became strictly a companion.

Ch. Artistic Dainty Doll from 1945. By the 1930s, the above-seven-pounds category had been elimi-nated.

The English Background

The first Pomeranians brought into England came from a northeast corner of Germany called Pomerania. Although they are named after it, Poms did not develop in this province, but actually originated in southern Germany.

Occasionally these larger Pomeranians whelped a litter that contained a sport: an extra-small puppy. At matu-rity these puppies weighed about ten to twelve pounds, a drastic difference from the thirty-pound parents. The adorable appearance of the sports created an interest in them. This led to intentional breeding for the smaller size, but it wasn't until the Victorian era that serious efforts to breed a smaller version started.

Queen Charlotte, wife of King George III, probably became acquainted with the breed during her childhood in a neighboring duchy of Pomerania. Recognizing a fellow royal, she brought the breed into her fold, and by 1761 Pomeranians romped in the court of King George III.

Charlotte's children also appreciated the breed. Her daughters owned several white-colored Poms that weighed in the twenty- to thirty-pound range. Queen Charlotte's son, the Prince of Wales, had a beautiful black-and-white Pom named Fino.

Then, in 1888, Great Britian's Queen Victoria, on tour in Florence, Italy, obtained a red sable Pomeranian called Marco. He weighed around twelve pounds, which at that time was regarded as a small size, though it would be considered large by our current standards.

Popular and beloved Queen Victoria influenced her subjects like today's movie stars affect their fans. Her subjects wrote about and copied her every move, mode of dress, taste and hobby. So when she started exhibiting Marco in dog shows, his appearance and every aspect of his show career became of public interest. Victoria's subjects copied their queen and started acquiring Pomeranians, and the breed became quite fashionable as a ladies' pet.

Queen Victoria kept a large kennel of Pomeranians at Windsor and started exhibiting these dogs. Her interest helped promote the growth of dog shows. She kept Pomeranians with her until her death in 1901. By then the breed was well established in England and starting to become popular in the United States.

The public's interest in the diminutive version of the Pomeranian popularized by Queen Victoria led to deliberate breeding for the smaller size. Fanciers reduced size successfully, and by the 1890s the size of Pomeranians entered at English Kennel Club shows was much smaller. In 1896 two size categories appeared

FAMOUS OWNERS OF POMERANIANS

Fran Drescher

David Hasselhoff

Queen Victoria

Michelangelo

Isaac Newton

for Pomeranians: over eight pounds and under eight pounds. Eventually the categories changed to over or under seven pounds. Finally, as breeders successfully made the Pomeranian a toy dog, the over-seven-pound category disappeared altogether.

Pomeranians in the United States

The earliest mention of Pomeranians in the United States appeared in the late 1880s when the AKC registered the first one. The initial imports, large white Poms weighing around twenty to thirty pounds, came from England. At first fanciers brought them over for use in the showring, but the breed quickly spread throughout the United States to rule ordinary households.

Poms come in a great variety of colors.

In 1900 the American Kennel Club (AKC) recognized the Pomeranian with the result that, at dog shows, the Pom could now leave the miscellaneous classes and exhibit in the Non-Sporting Group. He remained in this group until the establishment of the toy group in 1928. The standard at this time, similar to England's, called for under- and over-eight-pound categories, so as late as the early 1930s the larger Pomeranians remained.

The same year that the AKC recognized the breed, Mrs. Frank Smyth and Mrs. Hartley Williamson founded the American Pomeranian Club (APC), and nine years later the club became a member of the AKC. They founded the club as a way to promote the breeding of purebred Pomeranians and to urge members to follow the APC Standard of Excellence in breeding.

The members of APC guard the breed standard and determine what changes, if any, occur in it. In 1911 the APC held its first specialty show. For the past thirty years this affair, held the day before the Westminster Kennel Club show, has taken place in New York.

History of Pomeranian Colors

During the late 1890s, Pomeranian coats were white, black, brown, blue, dark orange, beaver, cream, parti-color and shaded sable. As the breed became smaller the white color went out of favor. It is difficult to breed white Poms and still keep them small. The gene for a white-colored coat seems to be linked to the gene for a bigger size, and if you breed white dogs to white dogs, the offspring start to revert to a larger Pom with bigger ears and longer muzzles.

The flashy, brilliant, clear orange became the rage during this century, almost obliterating the other colors, and by the 1980s the other colors, except for orange sable, seemed to disappear. Fortunately, in the last ten years the trend reversed, and now it is common to see cream, cream sable, black, black and tan, parti-color and chocolate Poms; less so the beaver, blue and white colors, but they are out there. The wolf

WHERE DID DOGS COME FROM?

It can be argued that dogs were right there at man's side from the beginning of time. As soon as human beings began to document their own existence, the dog was among their drawings and inscriptions. Dogs were not just friends, they served a purpose: There were dogs to hunt birds, pull sleds, herd sheep, burrow after rats—even sit in laps! What your dog was originally bred to do influences the way it behaves. The American Kennel Club recognizes over 140 breeds, and there are hundreds more distinct breeds around the world. To make sense of the breeds, they are grouped according to their size or function. The AKC has seven groups:

1) Sporting, 2) Working,
3) Herding, 4) Hounds,
5) Terriers, 6) Toys,
7) Non-Sporting

Can you name a breed from each group? Here's some help: (1) Golden Retriever; (2) Doberman Pinscher; (3) Collie; (4) Beagle; (5) Scottish Terrier; (6) Maltese; and (7) Dalmatian. All modern domestic dogs (*Canis familiaris*) are related, however different they look, and are all descended from *Canis lupus*, the gray wolf.

sable, however, is extremely rare. When an advertisement lists this color, be assured these people do not know much about the Pomeranian. They confuse the normal grayish-brown puppy hue, which will mature to an orange color, with the black-tipped silver wolf sable color.

Today we can watch history in progress, because another color coats the Pomeranian. In British Columbia a chocolate female, bred to Dunn's Tomspotter, a red sable male, produced brindle-colored puppies. The high dominance of the gene should ensure an increasing growth of brindle-colored Pomeranians. This color in a long-haired Pom looks very unusual and those who have seen it either love it or hate it. The standard can be interpreted either for or against the pattern; some judges throw the brindles out of the ring, while others award them blue ribbons.

Some Poms Who Made History

Pomeranians started making inroads into obedience in 1940 when Champion Batman Bacheler won his CD and became the first Pomeranian to receive an Obedience title. A couple of years later, Georgian's Betty became the first Pomeranian to win all Obedience titles. She accomplished this feat in eight months and managed to get seven perfect scores of 200 points each. When the AKC established a championship category for Obedience competition, Uhland's Creme Puff Delight become the first OTCH in July 1977.

The Pom's small size doesn't deter her from being a stellar achiever. This one is competing in open agility.

In the showring, Champion Rider's Sparklin' Gold Nugget, a beautiful clear orange, ranks as the top winning Pomeranian of all time, with forty-one Bests-in-Show.

Pom lovers saw history made in the winter of 1988, when Champion Great Elm's Prince Charming II became the only Pomeranian to win Best-in-Show at the prestigious Westminster Kennel Club show. Anyone who doesn't believe the Pomeranian is a "Little King" obviously didn't see Prince strut at Madison Square Garden. Every step he took said, "I'm special," and as this tiny aristocrat did his royal walk, the large dogs in the ring, who should have overshadowed this four-and-a-half-pound mite, faded into the background.

The Pomeranian Today

From a beloved companion of royalty to the playmate of Ziegfeld girls, the Pom always mingled with the rich and famous, and today's Pomeranian follows this tradition. Poms appeared in the biographical movie *Liberace* and in the television series *The Nanny*. Champion Great Elm's Prince Charming II, the Pom

Today's Pomeranian is comfortably ensconced in homes around the country.

who won Westminster in 1988, topped his showring career with a stint in show business. For several years he starred in television commercials as a representative of a dog food company.

In appearance the modern Pomeranian resembles his ancestors, but at the same time he looks vastly different. Occasionally a larger dog of the older type may appear in a litter, but the breed today is truly a toy breed, and Poms usually weigh under seven pounds. He also comes in a variety of colors to satisfy every taste.

Regardless of color, the popularity of the Pomeranian flourishes. Bearing the title of "companion dog," he has left the cold halls of castles for the comfort of central heating and is now firmly ensconced in homes around the world.

chapter 3

The **World**
According to the
Pomeranian

A worthwhile king answers to his subjects, cares for them, maintains a military to protect them, and though not intentionally, entertains them with his foibles. The Pomeranian follows in the footsteps, or maybe I should say pawprints, of his royal forerunners. He feels he owns you. Your home is his realm, you are his subject, his focus, and like any good king, he has an obligation to love, protect and entertain his vassals.

"The Little King"

The Little King fulfills his responsibility by being the perfect companion. He starts out by living a long life, around fourteen to seventeen years, which means his person has more years of love and companionship with this breed than another larger variety. The Pom doesn't restrict his person's lifestyle. For example, he uses papers for a bathroom and doesn't make his person get up early for a potty walk; when they travel together, he helps his person by conveniently fitting under the airplane seat.

LOVING AND AFFECTIONATE

The Pom also gives lots of love to his subjects. Jumping around like a bouncing ball, he will greet you with ecstasy. He will lay next to you on the couch or at your feet in quiet fellowship or cuddle on your lap. Wherever you go in the house you will hear the little pat-pat of his feet as he follows you from room to room. After all, how can he take care of his subjects when he's not with them?

LOYAL AND PROTECTIVE

All good kings protect their subjects, and the Pomeranian takes this responsibility very seriously. The least sign of intrusion, the smallest sound, a hint of invasion from someone outside your home, will bring on a burst of furious indignation. He will charge around his realm warning with full voice, "Keep out of my kingdom, or else." When the imagined threat is over he puffs out his chest, struts about, clearly put out that someone would have the nerve to approach his territory. Of course, if the intruder turns out to be a visitor, his royal manners appear and he issues lots of kisses and wags to the guest. Regardless of how vocal his warnings get, the Pom's noble nature doesn't allow him to snap at or bite a visitor.

> ### CHARACTERISTICS OF A POMERANIAN
>
> energetic
>
> affectionate
>
> mischievous
>
> delicate
>
> confident

His hearing is so acute that you will never need an alarm system. If you have a larger dog in your household you will find that your Pom will hear sounds long before the other dog.

One Pom surprised his person by demonstrating radar-hearing. Tom started a business that required him to travel every day in his small plane. Not wanting to leave his beloved Pom alone, he started bringing Tipper with him. The dog adjusted to the plane and would curl up and sleep during the trips. Except, every once in a while he would jump up and bark furiously. Tom was completely baffled at Tipper's behavior, until he noticed that every time Tipper started barking another plane, previously out of sight, would appear.

He's Not Always Royal

Your Little King doesn't always act like a paragon of virtue, especially when young. You need to remember that a little prince or princess can get into trouble. How many times have you read about royal sons keeping company with females of questionable repute or racing cars too fast? Keep a close eye on your little Pom while he is young. A few of mine have had my walls for dinner and my linoleum floors for dessert.

The Pom loves to curl up in the lap of his favorite person.

Take notice that the Pomeranian's working background will occasionally pop up. More than one member of the American Pomeranian Club has reported that they own a Pom who loves to herd ducks or chickens. Using appropriately sized sleds, teams of Pomeranians in the late 1980s proved that they still can do the job when they demonstrated sled-pulling at APC Specialty shows.

There are Poms who love to do serious work. The best example is hearing-assistance dogs, another is tracking.

Yep, you read it right—tracking. Our pampered lap-dog with the royal attitude will leave his soft couch and warm hearth for the outdoor life. Many a Pointer or Labrador has watched flabbergasted as a tiny Pom, on his way to a Tracking title, charged through shoulder-high weeds, jumped woodchuck carcasses, ignored skunks and flushed birds and bunnies. A few larger dogs watched a Pom by the name of Spunky live up to his name when he worked a track in fifteen-degree temperatures, with snow and thirty mph winds, all in eight minutes.

An Entertaining Character

In the history of England's royal family, many members have exhibited eccentric behavior. Perhaps this is a side effect of noble upbringing, because the tendency to display idiosyncrasies also appears in our four-legged king. The Pomeranian is a character, and his quixotic actions will give you many hours of entertainment.

Young Pomeranians may look like angels, but they can be full of mischief.

The best way to show you Pomeranian eccentricity is to describe a few Pom characters I have known. Casey, a beautiful golden-orange champion, loved his rubber pacifier, but not as a toy. He never played with or chewed it; instead he carried it in his mouth all day long. Torn between conflicting desires, he would reluctantly lay it down when he wanted to bark, but only for a few seconds.

27

Casey displayed another, and not very noble trait, called the *sneak attack*. He believed that top dog status belonged to him, but he only weighed four and a half pounds and his kennelmate, Gus, weighed five and a half pounds. Casey fought a few battles to establish his dominance over Gus, but always lost. He was not a good loser, and one day, when I bent over to pick up Gus, Casey saw his chance. He realized that his bigger kennelmate couldn't bite back, so he charged and chomped his teeth in Gus's thigh so hard that he pulled him out of my arms. A furious Gus landed on the floor ready to fight his assailant, but Casey, acting totally innocent, trotted away. After all, he knew he would get trounced in a fair fight.

Casey carried the pacifier around with him wherever he went.

Casey's cousin, Mary-Mary, and his son, Mikie, also practiced sneak attacks. Mary-Mary and Mikie lived in a household with another Pom, Jimmy. Mary-Mary only weighed three pounds, Mikie four, and Jimmy six. Mikie liked to stake out a special spot behind the couch, and if Jimmy came near he would rush out, and before Jimmy had a chance to defend himself, give a quick nip, then scoot back to safety.

Mary-Mary liked to sleep in her dog basket and didn't seem to mind if Jimmy came near her special spot, but she suffered attacks of jealousy whenever Jimmy received attention. When Mary-Mary's person, Marie, called Jimmy using a sweet-talking tone of voice, Mary-Mary would run to him, grab his thigh and give it a couple of quick shakes, then race back to her bed. Of course six-pound Jimmy would look down at his three-pound kennelmate with a you-gotta-be-kidding expression on his face.

Even well-trained Pomeranians can surprise you with their mischievous antics. Spunky, a Pom with multiple Obedience and Tracking titles, surprised his owner when he came streaking down the hall with toilet paper in his mouth and ran behind the couch. The paper, still connected to the roll in the bathroom, lay in a white strip along the hall, through the living room and around the furniture.

Brenda, Spunky's owner, seems to have Poms that like toilet paper. One day she left the bathroom door ajar as she took a shower and received quite a shock when she opened the shower curtain and found shreds of toilet paper floating everywhere. Lost in this cloud of white sat three Poms, trying hard to look innocent.

One quirk is universal to the breed. I call it the bezerker. Most Poms prefer to do the bezerker around a coffee table but if one is not available they will do it anywhere. Nothing in particular seems to start this behavior. One minute the Pom is standing still or walking calmly, and the next minute he lowers his head, arches his back, puts his tail really low, and starts to run at top speed in circles. His tongue, hanging out the side of his mouth, flaps in the wind; his jaws spread open in a smile of ecstasy; his eyes shine in delight. Round and around he goes until he drops in happy exhaustion.

Pomeranians are full of entertaining antics.

What Can You Expect from a Pomeranian?

NOT A PLAYMATE FOR SMALL CHILDREN

When you bring a Pomeranian into your household you can expect an entertaining and loving companion, but you cannot expect to get a dog that is a playmate for small children. He may look like a stuffed toy, but he is a living creature who has no defense from the energy of the very young child. Most reputable breeders will not sell a Pomeranian to a household with children under seven. The Little King may think he can, but his body is not built for the rough-and-tumble play of toddlers.

A Pom's intelligence, affection and cheerful humor are irresistibly endearing.

PET POMS SHOULD NOT BE BRED

You cannot expect to use a Pom for casual breeding. Pomeranians are called the heartbreak breed because so many things can go wrong when they deliver puppies. The female may not be able to deliver the puppies naturally and could die if veterinary help is not reached in time; you must be free to stay at home for at least seven days before her due date. The odds are high that she will need a C-section. If that happens, and she survives the anesthesia, her milk may be scarce or she may refuse to nurse the puppies. In that case, in order to save the puppies, you will have to tube-feed them every few hours around the clock for at least ten days.

You will find little difference between the sexes; the personality seems to be the same for both. The males do carry a fuller coat and shed less. Females shed near or after every season, unless spayed, in which case they will follow the same shedding pattern as a male. If you use your male dog for breeding, be prepared to deal with him lifting his leg and wetting in your house. Males used as a stud forget their housebreaking and rarely get it back.

Gets Along Well with Other Pets

You can expect the Pomeranian to get along well with other animals in the household, though you have to be careful to protect the Pom if you also own a larger dog. If the Pom feels the need to challenge the larger dog, he will do so regardless of the size of the other dog. Never leave them alone unsupervised.

The Pomeranian will often display a loving sensitivity toward his fellow creatures. Buffy and Sissy got along well with the black cat that lived with them. Except they would not allow the cat near their bed—never. One morning their person, Linda, got up and found the cat sleeping in Buffy and Sissy's bed with the two Pomeranians lying on the floor nearby. The lenient behavior of her dogs surprised Linda until she realized that her cat was ill. She took him to the vet and a few days later he died of kidney failure. Sensing the cat's illness, Buffy and Sissy had given her their special place to sleep.

An Intelligent Dog

The Pom is an intelligent dog and will use his smarts to solve problems

---

A DOG'S SENSES

Sight: With their eyes located farther apart than ours, dogs can detect movement at a greater distance than we can, but they can't see as well up close. They can also see better in less light, but can't distinguish many colors.

Sound: Dogs can hear about four times better than we can, and they can hear high-pitched sounds especially well. Their ancestors, the wolves, howled to let other wolves know where they were; our dogs do the same, but they have a wider range of vocalizations, including barks, whimpers, moans and whines.

Smell: A dog's nose is his greatest sensory organ. His sense of smell is so great he can follow a trail that's weeks old, detect odors diluted to one-millionth the concentration we'd need to notice them, even sniff out a person under water!

Taste: Dogs have fewer taste buds than we do, so they're likelier to try anything—and usually do, which is why it's especially important for their owners to monitor their food intake. Dogs are omnivores, which means they eat meat as well as vegetable matter like grasses and weeds.

Touch: Dogs are social animals and love to be petted, groomed and played with.

that arise in his dog world. For example, let me tell you about Sparky. Linda, his person, brought him home and trained him to go potty on newspapers. Sparky caught on to this concept quickly, and by the time he was twelve weeks old he faithfully ran to his paper whenever the urge hit him. Sparky matured at three pounds, so you can imagine how tiny he was at twelve weeks. One day Linda picked up the old papers and didn't immediately put out new ones from the pile she kept in her kitchen. Sparky trotted into the kitchen to use his potty and stood looking puzzled at his empty spot. He looked around and saw the foot-high pile of newspapers. Sparky walked over to the mound, studied it a few moments and then struggled up the stack until he was on top. He did his business and then hopped down. He didn't let a problem of height prevent him from doing the right thing.

To live with a Pomeranian is to live with a dog of contrasts. He gives love, affection and loyalty in a deferential manner, yet at the same time radiates demanding arrogance. His body is small, his bones fragile, yet, if challenged, he will take on a Rottweiler. A happy-go-lucky lapdog, the playboy of the dog world, he will leave his privileged life to serve the deaf, herd ducks, track or work in obedience.

The best way to describe the world according to the Pomeranian is to say that the Pom is unique, and his world is special because he is in it.

MORE INFORMATION ON THE POMERANIAN

The American Pomeranian Club
Jane Lehtinen
1325 9th Street South
Virginia, MN 55792

BOOKS

Hughes, Pauline B. *The Pomeranian*. Fairfax, Va.: Delinger's Publishers, 1990.

Pisano, Beverly. *Pomeranians*. Neptune City, N.J.: TFH Publications, 1990.

Teitjen, Sari B. *The New Pomeranian*. New York: Howell Book House, 1987.

MAGAZINES

The Pomeranian Review
The Official Publication of the American
Pomeranian Club
102 Tudor Lane
Lansing, MI 48906

The Pom Reader
8848 Beverly Hills
Lakeland, FL 33809-1604

VIDEOS

American Kennel Club. *Pomeranians*.

Living

with a

part two

Pomeranian

chapter 4

Bringing Your
Pomeranian
Home

A little advance planning will help you enjoy your Pomeranian puppy and keep him happy, healthy and safe.

What You Will Need

CRATES

A properly used crate will facilitate housebreaking, protect the dog from harm and give him a sense of security. Crates come in two types: wire cage and high-impact plastic with vented sides. The plastic crates are less expensive, lighter weight, more portable and better looking. However, the puppy would spend a large portion of his day in a dark environment. A wire crate gives him access to normal lighting conditions and also lets him experience the family surroundings. Although the wire cage works better in the house, its bulk and weight is impractical for transporting the dog. Ideally, you need both types. Use the wire crate for the house and the plastic for traveling.

Trainers recommend small crates for housebreaking purposes, but I could never bring myself to confine my puppies in such a small area. A slightly larger crate works just as well and is better for the dog. After all, for the first six months of his life he spends a lot of time in this crate. A wire crate, 17 1/4" x 24" x 20" high, allows enough space for a bed at one end and paper at the other. The puppy will automatically relieve himself in the area farthest from his bed. Therefore, he gets used to going on paper, and when he moves out of the crate he takes the habit with him. If you prefer to train the dog to go outside, using the larger size cage may delay housebreaking, but in time he will stop relieving himself in his crate altogether.

A wire crate lets your puppy experience her surroundings.

A cage with a lifting top makes it easy to clean up after the puppy, but a word of warning: A Pom can push up a loose top, and then when he lowers his body his head gets caught. Either keep the top open or, if you close it, make sure you hook it on securely.

Choose a plastic crate in a size appropriate for the adult Pom—not the puppy. Pick a crate with dimensions in the 16" x 21" x 15" high or 16 1/4" x 24" x 14" high range. One last note about plastic crates; in the car they can easily tip over, so secure them with the seat belt.

BEDDING

Pet shops offer a wide variety of attractive dog beds with unattractive prices. You can create an inexpensive alternative by purchasing a plastic kitty litter pan. Toss in some bedding, such as fake lambskin or towels, and you have a long-lasting, handsome bed that is easy to keep clean.

LEASH AND COLLAR

A collar can wear down the ruff around the Pomeranian's neck. To reduce this wear and tear use an eight-inch, fine-weight nylon martingale lead with chain. This leash may be difficult to find, as most pet shops don't carry it, but the shop owner may be able to order one for you. If you are unable to get a martingale, use a woven nylon, flat web, five-eighths-inch collar with matching lead. In addition, you may want to try a self-retracting leash for walking the dog.

WATER AND FOOD DISHES

A dish for eating and drinking can be as simple as a bowl from your kitchen or an elaborate ceramic dish from the pet shop. Just remember to keep water available at all times, especially for a Pom on a dry food diet. To prevent spillage, use a water dish that clamps on the side of the wire crate or a stainless steel nontip bowl.

IDENTIFICATION

Tags, tattoos and microchips all provide identification of your dog. The effectiveness of tags depends on your ability to keep them on the dog at all times. A tiny microchip placed in your dog's shoulder area needs a special machine to detect its presence, and until these machines become universal, the practicality of microchips ranks low. Presently the permanence and

**PUPPY
ESSENTIALS**

Your new
puppy will
need:

food bowl

water bowl

collar

leash

I.D. tag

bed

crate

toys

grooming
supplies

recognizability of tattooing delivers the best method of identification.

TOYS AND CHEWIES

Your Pom will love the latex squeaky toys, but keep a watch on him to make sure he doesn't remove the squeaker and choke on it. Fake lambskin toys are also a good choice. With the exception of pressed ground rawhide, the Pomeranian can choke to death on rawhide, so only give him the large knucklebone style, and remove it as soon as it starts to soften. Better yet, don't give him any rawhide at all. Cow hooves smell like a barnyard but remain the safest choice for the toy breed.

Pomeranian puppies are adorable, but make sure they aren't over-whelmed by activity and attention at first. Give them time to get adjusted.

Bringing Your Puppy Home

Before you pick him up make sure you have Nutrical or corn syrup in the house. (See Chapter 7, "Keeping Your Pomeranian Healthy," for more information on hypoglycemia.) On the way to your home he may get carsick, so bring paper towels with you. Ask the breeder for some of his dog food, and feed him this food for the first week or so. Change to another food gradually by adding a small amount of the new food and increasing this amount daily.

When you get him home everyone will want to touch or hold the puppy. Don't overdo it. Especially don't allow children in the household to handle him a lot. Let them pet his head or touch him in the crate, reserving more activity for a few days later. The stress of leaving his littermates and adjusting to a strange environment will strain this little baby. Cuddle and play with him but also give him plenty of rest.

Give your Pom a variety of toys to play with.

Too much play, combined with the stress of a new environment, may trigger a life-threatening hypoglycemic episode. For the first forty-eight hours you might want to add one-fourth teaspoon of white corn syrup to one-half cup of his drinking water. Do not use this mixture for more than two days, or you may cause the blood sugar problems that you're trying to avoid.

THE FIRST MONTH

During this period your puppy will spend a large portion of his time in the crate. Don't isolate him by putting the crate in a room away from the family. Place the crate in the kitchen where he can see and hear all the normal everyday activities. This helps him to become a better-adjusted adult. Give him plenty of toys to play with; put them in his crate one at a time, and when he gets tired of one remove it and put in another.

Make the kitchen puppy-friendly. Place all houseplants where he can't reach them, and remove all hazardous and poisonous materials. Close off all areas where he can reach electrical wires, including the space behind the refrigerator.

HOUSEBREAKING

Make a decision about the housebreaking method you want to use. You can train him to go potty outside, or you can paper train him to use a potty station in the house. The latter choice gives you the freedom to sleep late on a Sunday morning or to spend an evening at the movies without worrying that you have to get back home to let the dog out. Create the station in a corner of the kitchen or another easily accessible area, on tile or linoleum flooring. An eight-week-old puppy cannot hold his urine long enough to find a potty station in another room, so place the bathroom area near him.

Housebreaking will go smoothly if you don't give him the run of the house. Restrict him to one room, such as the kitchen. Place a board no higher than twelve inches across the door opening. Allow him to get within two feet of it and then slam the board down on the floor and yell, "No." Do this a couple of times and he will stay in the kitchen and never jump over the board. It is a lot easier to step over this board than opening a gate every time you need to go into the room.

Read the chapter on training (Chapter 8) and start the fundamentals of housebreaking and leash training. Also start getting him used to the grooming process by brushing him and handling his feet. Read the section on nails in Chapter 6 "Grooming Your Pomeranian"; it gives instructions on how to cut toenails and what type of scissors you'll need.

HOUSEHOLD DANGERS

Curious puppies and inquisitive dogs get into trouble not because they are bad, but simply because they want to investigate the world around them. It's our job to protect our dogs from harmful substances, like the following:

IN THE HOUSE

cleaners, especially pine oil

perfumes, colognes, aftershaves

medications, vitamins

office and craft supplies

electric cords

chicken or turkey bones

chocolate

some house and garden plants, like ivy, oleander and poinsettia

IN THE GARAGE

antifreeze

garden supplies, like snail and slug bait, pesticides, fertilizers, mouse and rat poisons

41

CAREFUL UNDERFOOT!

During this first month, you need to make him foot-wise. A Pom puppy running under your feet not only endangers him, but can cause you to take a nasty fall.

To avoid this problem, start teaching him to stay away from your feet. When you place him on the floor, slide your feet rather than walk, and when he gets near you, gently bump him with your foot or press on his toes very gently with your foot. Make this just unpleasant enough that he learns to avoid your feet. During the Pomeranian's lifetime he will be exposed to many human feet, and most of the time the human attached to them will not be aware of his presence. The dog must learn to protect himself.

As an owner of a toy breed, you will deal with safety problems that a large breed owner doesn't need

A small Pomeranian must learn early on to keep clear of people's feet.

to think about. Objects on the kitchen counter or table can fall on your Pom. For instance, a can of green beans could prove fatal if it fell on his head, so be aware, and keep objects away from counter and table edges.

FROM THREE TO SIX MONTHS

During this stage he will be learning and changing rapidly. As soon as he goes on the papers, allow him to stay out of the crate for longer periods of time. Leash-train him, then take him into the rest of the house. Put the leash on him and walk to the board, remove it, tell him "Okay," then lead him out of the kitchen. Keep an eye on him to make sure he doesn't potty in a forbidden area. When he starts running back to the kitchen to go on the papers, you can give him the run of the house.

The Pomeranian gets enough exercise just from normal household living. However, he needs fresh air and sunshine, so give him a daily romp on the lawn. Never tie an unsupervised Pomeranian outside; not only can he strangle on the lead, but larger dogs can prey on him.

From four to five months he will start teething, and you need to supervise him to avoid destruction of your property. I used to think that a small Pom could not do any damage until one chewed a hole through my kitchen wall. Buy cow hooves for him to chew on, and read the sections about teeth in Chapter 6 ("Grooming Your Pomeranian") and Chapter 7 ("Keeping Your Pomeranian Healthy").

*Let your Pom
have a daily
romp outside.*

Between four and five months, your gorgeous little fluff ball gets what Pom fanciers call the uglies. His legs get tall and gangly and his coat becomes short and ragged with long wisps sticking out like Phyllis Diller's hair before her makeover. Sometimes one part of the head will grow faster than the other and he will look strange, but don't despair, the ugly duckling will eventually turn into a swan.

The male Pom will start lifting his leg at around five months old. You may want to give the paper-trained dog a pee-post. Take a two-liter soda bottle and fill it half full of water, wrap newspaper around it, fasten with a rubber band, and put the post in the middle of his papers.

SIX MONTHS TO ADULTHOOD

His adult coat will start growing in along the top of his back and you will start to see his adult coloring. The uglies disappear and your Pom will look gorgeous again until he reaches twelve months, when he will go through the year-old shed. Refer to Chapter 6, "Grooming Your Pomeranian," for information on how to deal with this type of shed.

THE ADULT POMERANIAN

The Pom matures at around a year old and usually lives a long life. At this age, depending on his behavior, he may need to be crated when you leave the house, but other than that, he should be free most of the time.

The older Pom may become forgetful, develop arthritic bones, have vision problems and lose his teeth. He needs routine, so keep changes to a minimum. If arthritis makes grooming uncomfortable, trim his coat and keep it about one inch in length. Weight control, along with yearly checkups, will help preserve his health. You will have many wonderful years with your Pomeranian, and when that time of departure comes, let him go gently.

chapter 5

Feeding
Your
Pomeranian

Supermarket and pet store shelves bulge with a smorgasbord of dog foods, and they all proclaim superior nutrition. Exalted advertising makes it difficult to know what kind of food to use. Understanding the differences between the varieties of dog foods and learning to read labels, will make it easier for you to make knowledgeable choices.

How to Read a Label

The most important information on the label is whether or not the food is adequate to meet all of the dog's nutritional needs. Look for the words "complete and balanced nutrition" or the words "100 percent nutritionally complete." Never use any food that does not contain these words unless you are specifically using the food as a supplement or treat.

Look for the section that says "Guaranteed Analysis." The analysis gives you the minimum percentages for protein, fat, fiber, moisture, calcium, phosphorus and linoleic acid. These percentages vary for each brand of food and for each variety in a brand. Compare a maintenance dry food purchased from a pet store with protein at 26 percent, fat 16 percent, with a maintenance dry food from a supermarket with protein at 21 percent, fat 8 percent, and you can see that the second food does not supply enough fat for the young, active Pomeranian. You also can see why reading labels is important.

Next look at the part of the label that lists the ingredients. They are listed in descending order by weight, so if the label lists "turkey, barley, corn gluten meal, corn," you know that turkey is the primary ingredient in this dog food. Now let's compare these ingredients with a puppy kibble purchased at a supermarket. The ingredients listed are: "corn, corn gluten meal, rice, meat and bonemeal." Grains are the primary ingredient of this dog food. By comparing labels you can see that the puppy food from the supermarket doesn't supply the high-quality protein that the Pomeranian needs.

HOW TO READ THE DOG FOOD LABEL

With so many choices on the market, how can you be sure you are feeding the right food for your dog? The information is all there on the label—if you know what you're looking for.

Look for the nutritional claim right up top. Is the food "100% nutritionally complete"? If so, it's for nearly all life stages; "growth and maintenance," on the other hand, is for early development; puppy foods are marked as such, as are foods for senior dogs.

Ingredients are listed in descending order by weight. The first three or four ingredients will tell you the bulk of what the food contains. Look for the highest-quality ingredients, like meats and grains, to be among them.

The Guaranteed Analysis tells you what levels of protein, fat, fiber and moisture are in the food, in that order. While these numbers are meaningful, they won't tell you much about the quality of the food. Nutritional value is in the dry matter, not the moisture content.

In many ways, seeing is believing. If your dog has bright eyes, a shiny coat, a good appetite and a good energy level, chances are his diet's fine. Your dog's breeder and your veterinarian are good sources of advice if you're still confused.

Types of Dog Foods

Dry foods store easily, cost less, digest well and supply adequate nutrients. A Pomeranian can live a full, healthy life and never eat anything but dry dog food. Dry kibble also has the added benefit of lessening tartar accumulation. However, there are a couple of downsides to dry food. First, dogs don't like it as well as other kinds of food. That makes sense if you think about it; the natural diet of the canine is not a dry biscuit but moist, flesh food. Second, some dry foods may lack sufficient high-quality protein and fat to meet the needs of a toy breed, especially if you use a supermarket brand that contains a large amount of vegetable protein. Select a maintenance dry food that does not go below 25 percent protein and 12 percent fat, with higher percentages in puppy food. Make sure the label says, "balanced and complete." Check the ingredients and only purchase foods that list a flesh-food protein, such as turkey, chicken, meat meal or lamb, as one of the first two ingredients.

A puppy will need small servings of food several times daily; the older Pom will be happy with a larger meal once a day.

Canned dog food is more palatable to the Pomeranian, and if you only have one Pom the cost is minimal. If you have multiple dogs, dry food is more economical. The meat in canned food may consist of kidneys, tongue, liver or brain, along with skeletal muscle. Not all canned foods are complete and balanced;

some only contain meat, so it is important that you read the labels. A dog on a diet of canned food, with beef as the only ingredient, would soon become seriously malnourished. Make sure that meat or poultry is listed as one of the first two ingredients, that a cereal grain is included, and that the moisture content is not over 78 percent.

Pomeranians fed a diet consisting only of canned food may find tartar buildup a problem. By combining dry food with the canned you get the best of both types. Pour hot water over the dry kibble. Do not soak but pour off immediately, then mix one-fourth canned food to three-fourths dry.

Semimoist foods are full of corn syrup and some Poms may have adverse reactions to the food coloring it contains. I have tried feeding semimoist food to my dogs without success. They always threw it up. There are plenty of dog foods, without food dyes and other additives that are better choices for your pet.

Table scraps, contrary to popular opinion, are not necessarily bad for your dog. The problem is what type you choose and the amount you feed. Cookies, ice cream and fatty foods make the Pom overweight without supplying needed nutrients. Their palatability will cause him to eat less dog food, which results in an unhealthy diet.

Pomeranians love yogurt, cottage cheese, chicken, cucumbers, broccoli, tomatoes, green peppers, carrots, apples and grapes. All of these choices are healthy and make

TYPES OF FOODS/TREATS

There are three types of commercially available dog food—dry, canned and semimoist—and a huge assortment of treats (lucky dogs!) to feed your dog. Which should you choose?

Dry and canned foods contain similar ingredients. The primary difference between them is their moisture content. The moisture is not just water. It's blood and broth, too, the very things that dogs adore. So while canned food is more palatable, dry food is more economical, convenient and effective in controlling tartar buildup. Most owners feed a 25% canned/75% dry diet to give their dogs the benefit of both. Just be sure your dog is getting the nutrition he needs (you and your veterinarian can determine this).

Semimoist foods have the flavor dogs love and the convenience owners want. However, they tend to contain excessive amounts of artificial colors and preservatives.

Dog treats come in every size, shape and flavor imaginable, from organic cookies shaped like postmen to beefy chew sticks. Dogs seem to love them all, so enjoy the variety. Just be sure not to overindulge your dog. Factor treats into her regular meal sizes.

good additions to the Pomeranian's diet. One quick warning about grapes: A Pom will gulp them down, and they can lodge in his throat. To avoid this problem, bite the grape or smash it flat before giving it to your dog.

If you mix table scraps in the dog food, you will soon have a major problem on your hands. If mixed with dry food, the Pom will pick out each piece of kibble, lick it clean, then refuse to eat it. If mixed with moist food, he will refuse the whole mixture, and go on a hunger strike. It doesn't matter how hungry he gets or how much weight he loses, a Pom intent on forcing you to feed him only people food is stubborn as a mule. Believe me, he will outlast you. You can avoid this problem by feeding him his usual dog food at his regular time and save the table scraps for a treat. Except for yogurt or cottage cheese, don't put people food in a dog dish, but offer it from your fingers, and remember, only give him a tiny amount.

Another problem with table scraps is that they are usually offered to the dog while the family is eating at the table. This is understandable because you love your pet and want to share the goodies with him. Feed him from the table once or twice, and you will never again eat dinner in peace. At first the pressure of tiny paws will rest on your knees gently, but if you don't come through, then these soft paws will scratch indignantly on your leg. If you are still able to resist his endeavors he will then bring out the big ammunition—those brown, melting eyes. I don't know how the Pomeranian does it, but he can look at you with an expression that tugs at your heart in a way you can't resist. Somehow he will make you believe that he will starve to death, this very instant, if you don't give him some of your food. I have never known of a Pom owner who could resist, so it is better to never start the practice in the first place.

To use table scraps effectively keep the amount around 25 percent of the total diet, feed only healthy leftovers and never use table scraps as the only food for the dog.

Never mix them in with the dog food but feed them from your hand as a treat.

Nutritional Supplements

Complete and balanced dog foods include all essential vitamins and minerals. Dog food companies say that additional supplementation is not necessary and may throw off the balance of the diet. This is true; too much supplementation can be harmful, and I have gone years without giving my dogs added vitamins. However, when I added additional fat to my dogs' dry-food diet they stopped eating their stools, and when I added a one-a-day vitamin tablet the condition of their coats improved.

If you want to supplement your Pom's diet, first discuss it with your veterinarian, and never give more than the one-a-day vitamin tablet. This way you can supplement without endangering the dog. If you wish to add fat to the Pom's diet without throwing off the balance, only give one-eighth of a teaspoon.

Feeding Schedule

Dogs like routine, so you will avoid feeding problems by establishing a habitual eating schedule. The routine creates body rhythms that tell him to become hungry when his dinnertime approaches. Each day use the same food, dish, place and time.

Give him the food and only leave it down for thirty minutes. If he doesn't eat it, remove the food and do not feed him until his next scheduled feeding time.

HOW MANY MEALS A DAY?

Individual dogs vary in how much they should eat to maintain a desired body weight—not too fat, but not too thin. Puppies need several meals a day, while older dogs may need only one. Determine how much food keeps your adult dog looking and feeling her best. Then decide how many meals you want to feed with that amount. Like us, most dogs love to eat, and offering two meals a day is more enjoyable for them. If you're worried about overfeeding, make sure you measure correctly and abstain from adding tidbits to the meals.

Whether you feed one or two meals, only leave your dog's food out for the amount of time it takes her to eat it—10 minutes, for example. Freefeeding (when food is available any time) and leisurely meals encourage picky eating. Don't worry if your dog doesn't finish all her dinner in the allotted time. She'll learn she should.

Feeding Your Puppy

Two to Three Months

Soak puppy-formula dry food in hot water until completely soft. Make a mixture of one-half soaked kibble and one-half canned puppy food. Feed three to four times a day. Once a day give him a teaspoon of cottage cheese and a puppy vitamin. Follow the instructions on the label for the proper vitamin dosage.

The right food in the right amount will help ensure a healthy, active lifestyle for your Pom.

Three to Five Months

Feed the same as above but cut the feedings down to three times a day. Slowly decrease the added liquid until the kibble is barely moistened so that by the end of five months you're pouring hot water on the food, then immediately pouring it off. Mix in the canned food at a ratio of one-fourth canned to three-fourths dry.

Six Months to One Year

Continue serving the puppy formula but cut the feedings down to twice a day. Do not add water to the kibble, so that the puppy is now eating the same, with the exception that he is on puppy formula as an adult. When he reaches one year of age you can, if you choose, switch to a maintenance formula. Some food

51

manufacturers recommend that toy breeds remain on puppy formula for life. Remember the toy dog has a slightly higher metabolic rate. I like the size of the puppy kibble so I keep all my dogs, even the ten-year-old, on puppy formula.

Feeding the Adult Pomeranian

Once a day feed $^1/_4$ to $^1/_2$ cup dry dog food. (Protein no less than 25 percent, fat 12 percent and balanced and complete.)

TO SUPPLEMENT OR NOT TO SUPPLEMENT?

If you're feeding your dog a diet that's correct for her developmental stage and she's alert, healthy-looking and neither over- nor underweight, you don't need to add supplements. These include table scraps as well as vitamins and minerals. In fact, a growing puppy is in danger of developing musculoskeletal disorders by oversupplementation. If you have any concerns about the nutritional quality of the food you're feeding, discuss them with your veterinarian.

Stir in one teaspoon of a balanced and complete canned dog food.

Add a teaspoon of corn oil. (Optional)

One multi-vitamin mineral tablet. (Optional)

Once or twice a week substitute cottage cheese for the canned food.

Add healthy treats if so desired but never exceed one-fourth of the total daily food.

Or feed a diet of dry food only, and give a teaspoon of cottage cheese several times a week as a supplement.

Feeding the Older Pom

Stay with the same brand you have been using but switch to the senior formula.

Unsafe Food

To help keep your dog energetic and healthy, don't feed him sweets. Avoid giving him spicy or greasy snacks, and bypass dangerous foods such as chocolate, which can kill a dog, and foods that he can choke on, like french fries and peanut butter.

chapter 6

Grooming
Your
Pomeranian

A simple weekly routine can keep your Pomeranian clean, neat and free of tangles. Besides having cosmetic benefits, grooming can be a pleasant experience for your dog and will strengthen the bond between you.

Supplies

The minimum supplies needed are: a pin brush, a slicker brush, a metal comb made for dogs, four-inch ball-tipped scissors, and cat nail clippers. You also will need baby powder, a plastic spray bottle and grooming spray. Talcum powder can be dangerous for your Pom to breathe, so make sure the baby powder you buy is made of 100% cornstarch. For a grooming mist, use plain water or one of the following mixtures.

53

Mixture one:

One tablespoon of cream rinse. Get the kind made for dogs.

Eight ounces of water.

Mix ingredients together and fill the spray bottle.

Mixture two:

One to two tablespoons of Eau de Quinine Compound Hair Tonic by Ed Pinaud. This is a men's hair tonic, bright red in color, that can be purchased in most drugstore chains.

Six ounces of water.

A dash of witch hazel. (Optional)

This mixture is used by many professional handlers and it is the one I prefer. It cleans the coat and has a lovely fragrance. I have never known the red color to stain a dog's coat, but if your Pom is white, you might find that the first mixture is a better choice.

Brush your Pom at least once a week to keep him looking his best.

Brushing

Unless he has an unusually heavy coat, your Pom only needs to be brushed once a week. Never brush a dry coat, as this will break off the ends of the hair. Use the spray bottle filled with plain water or one of the grooming mixtures. Before you start brushing, dust some of the baby powder behind the ears and leave it there. This soaks up the oil that builds up in this area. I use a grooming table to brush my dogs, but if you don't have one, don't worry; your lap will work just as well.

Find a comfortable chair, cover your legs with a towel, and lay the dog in your lap. Put the dog on his side, head toward your knees, rump toward your body. Spritz some water or grooming mixture on him and, starting near the rump, separate the hair until you see the skin. Hold the top section down with one hand, and brush the bottom section in the direction the hair grows. Move up an inch and separate another section of hair, and repeat. Keep moving forward an inch or so until you have brushed his whole side. Repeat on the other side, then place him on his back. If you have a male, moisten the gummy area on his belly with the spray, then powder heavily and brush out the powder with the slicker brush. You may have to spritz and powder this area more than once. When finished, switch back to the pin brush and groom the chest, under the legs, his back and the breast area under his chin.

Brush the hair toward the face for a fluffed-up appearance.

Change over to the slicker brush and brush out the baby powder around the ears. If you find tangles, use your fingers to pull them apart, and starting near the skin, cut through the matt out to the end of the hair. Use the metal comb to remove the cut sections.

Finally, switch back to the pin brush, mist his coat and lightly brush his whole body, going against the grain and fluffing his hair toward his head. Put him on the floor and he will give a shake that settles each hair in place.

Trimming

The Pom can get feces stuck in his coat. To avoid this, take the blunt scissors and trim a small area, about one inch in diameter, around the anal opening.

When the hair between the Pom's toes becomes too long it interferes with his ability to walk on slippery floors. Turn the dog over on his back, and using the blunt scissors, carefully cut the hair between the toes.

Stand your Pom on a table or other hard surface, and, trimming around the foot, remove the tuft of hair that grows in front of the toes. Some pet owners leave this tuft, while others prefer the look of the trimmed foot.

Depending on your preference, the hair on the tips of the ears can be left natural or trimmed. Place the Pom in a sitting position with his head facing you. Grasp the ear at the top, putting the ear leather between your thumb and first finger. Make sure you are covering the ear-tip with your fingernails. Cut straight across the tip, then cut, at a slight angle downward, one-quarter inch on each side. Repeat on the other ear.

Use a table or other raised surface for grooming.

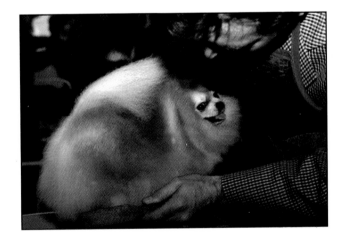

Bathing

If you brush your Pom once a week, you should rarely have to give him a bath. If a bath does become necessary, you can bathe him in your kitchen sink. He may become frightened of the slippery bottom, so put a rubber mat under his feet. Before you place your dog in the sink, turn on the water and adjust the temperature. Using the sink hose, wet him down until his coat is saturated. One word of warning: If this is the first time you're bathing your Pom, expect to have a good laugh, because your little fluff ball is going to look like a drowned rat.

A clean, well-groomed Pom is a pleasure to look at.

After he is thoroughly wet, move the running faucet out of his way but do not turn it off. It is difficult to adjust the water temperature with a wet soapy Pom in the sink, so once you have the warm/cold ratio correct, let the water run during the whole bath. Sometime during the wetting process the Pom will try to shake his wet coat. When this happens, grab the skin at the base of his neck and he will stop shaking.

Start at the neck area and apply enough shampoo to work up a lather. Be careful not to get any in his eyes. Work the lather into the hair and then thoroughly rinse. Wrap him in a thick towel and wipe off all excess water. Use a paper towel to wipe away any moisture in his ears, then blow-dry the coat.

Except for the insecticidal brands, your choice of shampoo is a matter of personal choice. They are all excellent. Strong flea shampoos can harm the tiny Pom, so it is important that you follow the directions on the label, and use insecticidal shampoos purchased from pet stores or your veterinarian, rather than supermarkets. Never use a shampoo designed for human use on your Pom, as this can cause his skin to become dry and itchy.

Blow-Drying

The Pomeranian's coat must be blown dry—even in the summer. The undercoat is too thick to dry quickly, and in hot humid weather a wet undercoat can cause hot spots to develop.

Place your dog on your lap, hold the hair dryer about ten inches away from his body, and, taking care to avoid his face, blow-dry the coat for about two minutes. Turn the dryer off and brush him with the pin brush, then blow another few minutes, and brush again. Keep this up until he is dry. This takes about thirty minutes. The dog will be scared of the dryer and he may try to jump off your lap, so hold on to him tightly. After a while, especially if you bathe your Pom often, he will get used to the dryer. Blow-drying is easier if you use a grooming table, a cage and table dryer. These items keep your hands free to brush while the dryer is blowing.

Nails

Trimming nails unnerves most new pet owners and many forego the task, instead asking their veterinarian to do the job. However, with a properly trained dog, cutting the nails is simple, safe and quick.

When cutting the nails, there's a natural tendency to squeeze the toe pads. This pressure causes the puppy to struggle, so he must get used to having his toe pads touched and squeezed. Lay the puppy on his back in your lap, with his head toward your knees, and gently compress each toe pad. If the puppy growls or tries to bite, gently snap your finger under his chin and also give a firm verbal reprimand. Do not hit hard, just a small tap strong enough to get his attention. Handle his toe pads several times a day until he's trained to lay flat on his back and allows you to handle his feet.

When you're ready to cut his nails, use cat nail clippers and make sure you have styptic powder on hand. Most pet stores carry both items; if not, ask your vet for some. Lay the puppy in your lap, just as you did in training him, and grab a toe. Try to hold it firmly without squeezing the pad. Then, with the cat scissors, cut off the tip of each nail.

You can see the quick in light-colored toenails but not in the black ones. If you should cut the quick, and this is bound to happen to you eventually, just put a pinch of the styptic powder on the nail. This will stop the bleeding and also helps to prevent infection.

Teeth

Hard kibble and nylon chew toys should keep your Pom's teeth white, but sometimes it's not enough to do the job. For optimal tartar prevention, brush at least three times a week using an infant toothbrush or one made especially for dogs. You also can use a toothpaste made for dogs, but plain water will work as well. Just make sure you never use human toothpaste; it's bad for dogs.

Ears

During the weekly grooming, check the inside of your Pom's ears. If you see any kind of wax buildup or dark brownish discharge, refer to the section on ears in Chapter 7 for information on how to take care of the problem.

Shedding

**GROOMING
TOOLS**

pin brush

slicker brush

flea comb

towel

mat rake

grooming
glove

scissors

nail
clippers

tooth-
cleaning
equipment

shampoo

conditioner

clippers

The Pomeranian sheds between four and six months of age, and again when he is one year old. After that, the male sheds once a year, and the female at each season. Good grooming practices will keep these shedding episodes short.

Poms shed their coat in two different ways, and each type requires a different grooming method. Some Poms blow their coat all at once with large clumps of hair separating from the body. Brush out the clumps with the slicker brush, bathe, blow-dry and brush again. You must brush the dog before his bath. Otherwise, the undercoat will form feltlike matts. Repeat this process a week later and you should find that most of the shed is finished. When you sit down to brush the dog make sure you have a paper bag next to you for receiving the dead coat. Believe me, you will fill up this bag. I am always amazed at how much hair comes off of my tiny little Poms.

In the second type of shed, the hair doesn't clump but falls out continuously. Bathe the dog, blow-dry and for the next two weeks brush daily. Don't make it a long process; just do a light brushing to pull out the dead hair. Other than the shedding period, fifteen minutes once a week is all the time needed to keep your Pomeranian well groomed.

chapter 7

Keeping Your
Pomeranian
Healthy

Books on dog health usually provide information appropriate for larger breeds and fail to make adjustments for the small— especially toy—dog. For instance, some books suggest using a men's necktie to muzzle an injured dog, or recommend giving a teaspoon of salt to induce vomiting. Try putting a necktie around the tiny Pom's muzzle— it doesn't work. Placing a teaspoon of salt on the back of a Pom's throat may choke him to death. In the middle of a crisis, you don't want to find out that you're acting on erroneous or

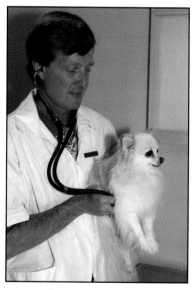

dangerous information, so, where appropriate, the health information in this chapter has been adapted to fit the toy breed.

Choosing a Veterinarian

No matter what the size of your dog, however, choosing a veterinarian is an important choice. Your Pom's veterinarian should be someone with whom you and your dog feel comfortable, who takes the time to communicate with you and who is knowledgeable about Pomeranians.

If possible, get a vet recommendation from your puppy's breeder, or talk to other Pom owners in your area.

YOUR PUPPY'S VACCINES

Vaccines are given to prevent your dog from getting an infectious disease like canine distemper or rabies. Vaccines are the ultimate preventive medicine: they're given before your dog ever gets the disease so as to protect him from the disease. That's why it is necessary for your dog to be vaccinated routinely. Puppy vaccines start at eight weeks of age for the five-in-one DHLPP vaccine and are given every three to four weeks until the puppy is sixteen months old. Your veterinarian will put your puppy on a proper schedule and will remind you when to bring in your dog for shots.

Vaccinations

If you stick to the schedule, vaccines are an easy way to protect your Pomeranian against several life-threatening diseases. Your Pom puppy will need to be vaccinated against distemper, hepatitis, parainfluenza, parvo and bordetella. Your puppy probably received some of his shots before you brought him home.

Some Poms react poorly to the leptospirosis vaccine, so mention this to your vet. You'll probably need to vaccinate your puppy at eight, twelve, sixteen and eighteen weeks of age, after which he'll need a yearly booster. At six months old, the rabies vaccine is usually given and a booster is given every two years thereafter. Discuss a vaccination schedule with your breeder and vet, and stick to it.

General Health Information

The following information is alphabetically arranged and cross-referenced.

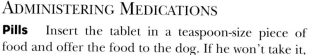

Pills   Insert the tablet in a teaspoon-size piece of food and offer the food to the dog. If he won't take it, open his mouth and place the pill on the back of his tongue. Hold his jaws closed, and with your free hand stroke his throat until you see him swallow.

Liquids   Fill an eyedropper, or oral syringe, with the correct dosage. Place your hand over the Pom's skull and hold his head still. With the jaws closed and his teeth clamped shut, insert the syringe in the side of the mouth between the back molars and the dog's cheek. Squeeze out a small amount of the medication, then stop and give the dog time to swallow. After he swallows squeeze out some more liquid. Repeat until finished.

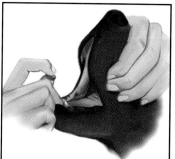

To give a pill, open the mouth wide, then drop it in the back of the throat.

Eye Medication   To administer eye-drops pull the lids apart and, holding the eyedropper about one inch from the eyeball, drop in the medicine. To apply an ointment pull the lower lid out, creating a little pocket, and squeeze in a bead of the ointment. Try to place the medicine on the inner lid rather than the eyeball.

Ear Medication   Hold the tube parallel to the head with the end of the tube pointing to the ceiling and the nozzle in the ear. Squeeze in the medication and massage the base of the ears.

Squeeze eye ointment into the lower lid.

ANAL GLANDS

The anal glands rest inside the anus on each side of, and slightly below the opening. These glands empty when the dog defecates, so don't routinely express them. Do so only when they feel full, or your dog starts scooting his rear end on the floor.

To empty the glands, take a clean facial tissue and place it over the opening. Feel the glands through the tissue, and with your fingers on one side of the anal opening and your thumb on the other, squeeze. The foul-smelling contents of the glands will squirt out onto the tissue. The secretion should be watery or have a soft, butterlike consistency. Hard lumps or thick pasty secretions suggest impaction. In this case you will need to get a veterinarian to empty the sacs. After expressing the anal contents, wipe the opening with baby wipes or a damp cloth.

Vaccinations are an easy way to make sure your puppy is protected from extremely dangerous diseases.

Infected glands will cause pus-draining, open sores to break through the skin. Treat the infection with oral antibiotics. If a fissure along the anal opening occurs, the dog may need surgery.

ARTIFICIAL RESPIRATION

(See CPR and Artificial Respiration later in this chapter.)

BANDAGING

(See Cuts and Lacerations later in this chapter.)

BEE OR INSECT STINGS

Remove the bee's stinger with tweezers, then cover the bite with a mixture of bicarbonate of soda and water. If the dog shows signs of shock or allergic reaction, contact your veterinarian immediately.

BLEEDING

Minor bleeding   Press a couple of pieces of sterile gauze on the wound and apply firm pressure for a few minutes. When the bleeding stops, treat the area as you would for cuts and lacerations.

Major bleeding   Blood spurting out of a wound, instead of flowing, is an emergency, and you only have a few minutes to stop the bleeding. Grab a wad of rolled cotton, make a pack of sterile gauze pads, or even use a washcloth, and press firmly on the wound. Get vet help immediately, and if someone else can help, let them place a tourniquet on the leg while you're pressing on the wound.

Place the **tourniquet** between the wound and the heart. Take a strip of cloth, approximately $1^1/_2$ inches wide, place it above the wound and wrap it around the leg. Make one knot, then lay a stick, or something similar, on it. Tie a second knot over the stick. Turn the stick and tighten the strip of cloth. Hold or tie the stick in place. Make sure you release the tourniquet every fifteen minutes for a few moments, because if left on too long it can cause permanent damage to the leg.

CAR SICKNESS

To help the Pom adjust to the noise and motion of the car, take him out for short drives. Increase the distance each day until he becomes comfortable in the car. Sometimes it helps if you give him a dose of Pepto Bismol before you leave.

CHOKING

I have known Poms who have choked to death, one on a piece of chicken fat, another on dry kibble. In the second incident the Pom tossed a piece of dry dog food in the air, and when he caught it the food slipped past his teeth and lodged in his throat. One of my Poms died in front of me, choking on soaked kibble, while I struggled to get the food out of his mouth. Unfortunately, at that time I didn't know how to do the Heimlich maneuver or he could have been saved.

Signs of choking vary according to the type and severity of the suffocation. Gagging, trying to clear the throat and pawing at the mouth are all signs of a foreign object in the throat. Do not attempt the Heimlich maneuver if he makes any kind of sound, as this shows that he is getting air into his lungs. Instead, open his mouth and look for the obstruction. Using your fingers in a scooping motion, try to remove the object. If you cannot get it out, take him to a veterinarian immediately.

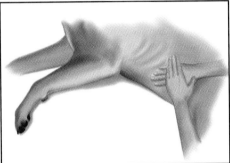

Applying abdominal thrusts can save a choking dog.

When the airway is totally obstructed, the dog cannot make any sound, and it is hard to see if he is choking. At first he freezes into a position with his head bent down. Then he will start to move, and will try to run to his crate or a similar safe place or he may stagger a few feet and collapse. In this urgent situation, he can die in minutes from lack of oxygen. Remain calm, and try to get the object out of his throat. If you are unable to scoop or pull out the obstruction, do the Heimlich maneuver.

Perform the **Heimlich maneuver** with the dog lying on his side. Spread your hands just below the ribs and apply several quick thrusts. If necessary, repeat the maneuver. Make sure you don't press on his ribs.

You may not always see it when your dog swallows an object or chokes, so anytime you observe him staggering, or if he collapses, always check his throat to see if there is an obstruction in it.

COUGHING

Reverse Sneeze   Many Pomeranians experience what is called reverse sneezing, where the dog clears his throat with a loud snorting noise. Contraction of the muscles in the throat cause this harmless problem. I have found that if I put a smidgen of honey on the top of the Pom's nose I can stop the spasm. The dog stretches out his tongue to lick off the honey and this motion seems to return the throat muscles to normal. However, when your dog coughs, don't automatically diagnose it as a reverse sneeze. A cough can be a signal of more serious problems and your veterinarian must first rule out these conditions.

Trachea Collapse Pomeranians are susceptible to a condition where the cartilage in the windpipe collapses, and the dog produces a honking type of cough. Most dogs can live fairly comfortably with this condition, especially if their weight is kept under control. However, in some cases the problem may be life-threatening and the dog must be monitored by a veterinarian.

Kennel Cough Suspect this problem if your Pom develops a frequent, dry, barking type of cough, especially if he recently stayed in a boarding kennel. While not a serious problem for adults, kennel cough can cause miscarriage in a pregnant dog and is hard on young puppies.

Other Types of Cough A chronic cough or clearing of the throat can indicate a heart problem. Frequently this type of cough occurs more often at night and after exercise. A cough accompanied by wheezing needs medical care, as it may be caused by an allergy or asthma.

CPR AND ARTIFICIAL RESPIRATION

Clean any mucus or obstructions out of the throat. Check his pulse (located on the rear leg where it attaches to the groin). If he has one, but he's not breathing, start **artificial respiration.** Hold his mouth closed, and for your comfort place a handkerchief, if available, over his nose and mouth. Put your mouth over his whole muzzle, and blow in tiny puffs of air using a count of: one one-thousand, two one-thousand, three one-thousand. Puff a breath of air on the single number and rest on the one-thousands. Remember the Pom has tiny lungs so don't blow a full breath, just enough to see his chest rise.

If the dog is not breathing and you can't find the heartbeat, start **CPR.** Lay the dog down on his right side. Put your hand over the chest in the area right behind his elbow and on the lower part of the chest. Press and release five times, then put your mouth over his muzzle and give one puff. Press and release the chest again for five times, then puff. Keep repeating. Do not press too hard on the ribs.

CUTS AND LACERATIONS

Pull the long hair out of the wound and cut the hair surrounding the injured area. Clean the wound with a soapy cloth and wash the area surrounding it. Rinse the soap out of the cloth and use the clean cloth to remove the soap from the injured area. Make sure you remove all traces of soap. After cleaning the area apply antibiotic ointment, and cover the cut with a bandage.

Bandaging: Bottom of Feet Clean the wound and put antibiotic cream on it. Tear a cotton ball apart, and put tiny slivers between the toes. Cut a two-inch strip of porous, adhesive tape, and lay it down with the sticky side up. Take a 4 x 4 inch sterile gauze pad and cut it in half. This gives you a piece about two inches wide by four inches long. Fold the pad in half and place it in the middle of the adhesive strip. Place the

---

A FIRST-AID KIT

Keep a canine first-aid kit on hand for general care and emergencies. Check it periodically to make sure liquids haven't spilled or dried up, and replace medications and materials after they're used. Your kit should include:

Activated charcoal tablets

Adhesive tape
(1 and 2 inches wide)

Antibacterial ointment
(for skin and eyes)

Aspirin (buffered or enteric coated, *not* Ibuprofen)

Bandages: Gauze rolls (1 and 2 inches wide) and dressing pads

Cotton balls

Diarrhea medicine

Dosing syringe

Hydrogen peroxide (3%)

Petroleum jelly

Rectal thermometer

Rubber gloves

Rubbing alcohol

Scissors

Tourniquet

Towel

Tweezers

dog's foot on top of the gauze and wrap the tape around the foot.

Take a strip of adhesive tape, and wrap from the rear along the bottom and toward the front of the foot, then up and over the exposed toes and over the top of the bandaged foot. Wrap adhesive tape, in a spiral pattern, around the bandaged foot, and up the leg to the wrist on the front leg, or midway between the foot and hock on the rear leg. Let the sticky adhesive hold the bandage on. A tight bandage can cut off the circulation in the dog's leg, so wrap the tape snugly, but not so tight as to constrict the blood flow.

The Pom will not like this bandage and may try to chew it off. Spray some bitter apple in a small dish, soak the ends of a cotton ball in the fluid, and swab the bitter apple on the tape. Do not saturate, just lay down a film of the fluid. This should prevent the dog from chewing on the bandage.

Leg   Cover the wound with a sterile gauze pad, and attach the pad with porous adhesive tape. Move the leg, and make sure that the leg can bend at the knee, wrist, pastern or hock.

Body   Trim hair around the wound and apply antibiotic ointment. Place a sterile gauze pad and tape it in place by laying strips of porous adhesive tape along the ends of the pad. Extend the tape a few inches past the pad.

DEATH

A dog becomes a member of his human family, and when he dies, whether by accident, illness or euthanasia, the loss tears a hole in his person's heart. Students at the University of California–Davis veterinary school offer a grief consulting line at 1-916-752-4200. You also may want to ask your vet to recommend a local grief consultant.

DEHYDRATION

Check for dehydration by pulling up the skin on the dog's neck and shoulder area and then letting go. This skin should snap back in place. If it returns slowly, the dog is dehydrated. Using the oral syringe, force water down the dog's throat, then call the veterinarian. The condition causing the dehydration must be treated. (See Administering Medications earlier in this chapter.)

DIARRHEA

To treat diarrhea use the oral syringe and give your Pom one-fourth teaspoon of Kaopectate per five pounds of body weight. Repeat this dose several times a day. Do not feed for twelve hours, then feed him a mixture of pablum and turkey or beef baby food. Keep him on this diet for two to three days. For young puppies also give one-fourth inch of Nutrical three times a day. Call the vet if the stool shows blood, the dog has a fever, the diarrhea continues for more than twenty-four hours or the dog becomes dehydrated.

DISTEMPER

The incubation period for this highly contagious viral disease ranges from three to fifteen days. One of the primary causes of deaths in dogs, distemper spreads by contact with infected animals. The illness unfolds with a fluid discharge from the eyes and nose which eventually turns thick and yellow; fever; muscle twitching and seizures. There is no effective treatment of distemper, but it can be prevented by routine vaccination.

EARS

Cleaning   The usual instruction for cleaning a dog's ears is to use a cotton ball or a piece of cloth wrapped around the finger. This doesn't work very well in the small Pomeranian ear, so use cotton swabs instead. If you put the swab down into the ear canal opening, you can damage the eardrum, so be careful. Just use common sense and don't go too deep into the ear.

To remove **wax** from the ear dip a cotton swab in peroxide, and press the swab against a napkin to remove excess fluid. Brush the wax in the ear with the damp swap and discard. Wipe the moistened wax out with dry swabs. This may take four or five swabs. After the wax is removed, dust the inside of the ear with ear powder and massage the base.

Keeping the ear dry helps prevent most ear problems. When spraying the dog with his grooming mist, make sure you do not spray into the ear. After a bath, wipe out the moisture with a paper towel or cotton swab.

Fungus Infections   If a musty-smelling, dark-brown discharge with no simultaneous itching fills the ear, suspect a fungus infection. Clean the ear as described above and see your vet for treatment.

Ear Mites   With ear mites the discharge is similar to the fungus discharge, but the dog suffers from itching. He will shake his head and scratch at his ears. Investigate by looking at the secretions under a microscope to see if white specks appear in the dark discharge. Do not treat this condition without a diagnosis from your veterinarian. Ear mite medications can make other ear problems worse, so make sure that your dog really has ear mites.

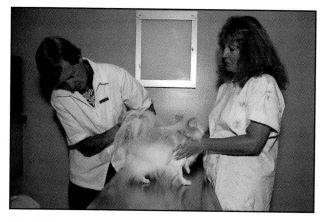

You can be a good judge of your Pom's health. Take her to the vet if you notice any unusual symptoms.

Ear Allergy   Itchy ears without a discharge indicate an allergy, especially if the skin looks red. See your veterinarian.

Ear Infections   With an external ear infection the Pom will shake his head, paw at his ear and walk around with the affected ear held at half-mast. Treat the infection with an antibiotic, prescribed by your

71

veterinarian. An inner-ear infection causes the Pom to lose his balance or walk in circles.

ELECTRIC SHOCK

The Pomeranian becomes a candidate for electric shock because he can easily reach the electrical wires behind furniture and appliances. Aside from burning the mouth, electric shock damages the lungs and causes them to fill with fluid. Check an unconscious Pom for breathing and give artificial respiration if necessary. If the only damage is a burned mouth, feed him a bland diet of soft food and check the membranes daily. If any of the membranes turn grey, take the dog to the veterinarian, as the dead tissue has to be removed.

EYES

It is not unusual for a Pom to get dust and other objects in his eyes. If your dog squints and paws at his eyes, open his eyelids and look for a foreign object. To remove the matter, put your forefinger above the eye and your thumb below and spread the lids apart, then squeeze them together. Repeat the action several times. This should force the foreign matter either to the side of the eye or bunch it up in the middle of the eyeball. Hold the eyelids open, and with a clean facial tissue gently wipe the excess material out. Do not touch the eyeball with the facial tissue, just the foreign material. This is easier to do than it sounds.

You also can remove objects by irrigating the eye with the isotonic saline solution. You can find this eyewash at most drugstores. If you cannot find a foreign object in the eye, pull the lower lid down and take a look at the membranes; they should be pink. Bright red tissues indicate an eye infection.

Some Poms develop a continuous runny eye that leaves a brown stain on the fur. Wash the stain off with a cloth saturated with warm water. Otherwise, the discharge will form a brown crust. Treat the discharge with long-term use of tetracycline.

First-Aid Kit

Acquire the following items and make a first-aid kit for your Pom. Aside from the usual things you need to have in a first-aid kit, you need to keep some special things on hand that are particular to your Pomeranian. Make sure you have artificial tears, isotonic saline eyewash, Nutrical (obtainable at pet stores or from your veterinarian), an oral syringe (ask your pet store or vet to order it for you) and two pieces of cloth: one one-and-a-half inches wide and twenty-four inches in length, the other an inch wide and twenty-four inches in length. Keep a small supply of human baby food; get barley or rice pablum and small jars of lamb or turkey.

Fleas

The Pomeranian's heavy undercoat makes it hard to detect fleas. During flea season, routinely check the top of his back under his tail. Tiny black specks are signs of infestation. Put the specks in water, and if they ooze blood, they are flea droppings. Fleas mate and lay their eggs on the dog's skin. These eggs drop off into the carpet, sofa or dog's bedding, and hatch into larvae.

Flea sprays do not work well on the Pom. The spray cannot penetrate the undercoat; therefore, it never reaches the fleas that live on him. Flea collars work but may produce too strong of an insecticide for the tiny Pom's safety, so check with your veterinarian before using a flea collar.

Treat the premises with a premise insecticide, wash the dog's bedding and bathe the Pom with a flea shampoo. After he is dry, dust him with flea powder. The powder stays down in the undercoat and

> ### FIGHTING FLEAS
>
> Remember, the fleas you see on your dog are only part of the problem—the smallest part! To rid your dog and home of fleas, you need to treat your dog *and* your home. Here's how:
>
> • Identify where your pet(s) sleep. These are "hot spots."
>
> • Clean your pets' bedding regularly by vacuuming and washing.
>
> • Spray "hot spots" with a nontoxic, long-lasting flea larvicide.
>
> • Treat outdoor "hot spots" with insecticide.
>
> • Kill eggs on pets with a product containing insect growth regulators (IGRs).
>
> • Kill fleas on pets per your veterinarian's recommendation.

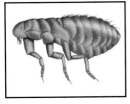

*The flea is a
die-hard pest.*

does an excellent job of flea prevention. Its gritty feel will wear off after a couple of days. During the flea season, repeat the powdering every seven days. In addition, ask your veterinarian for once-a-month prescription tablets (lufenuron tablets). These stop the flea life cycle at the egg stage.

Some dogs have allergic reactions to flea bites and will have severe itching that persists even after the pests are gone. A veterinarian can give you medication for treating the allergic reaction. Treat a bad flea bite as you would a wound.

GENITAL AND RELATED AREAS: FEMALES

Pyometra This infection of the uterus is a life-threatening condition, so you need to know the symptoms, or better yet spay your girl. Pyometra usually occurs in older females, but it also can occur in the younger Pom. The dog will act like she doesn't feel well; she will stop eating and her abdomen may be enlarged or feel hard when touched. In some cases a heavy, beige-colored discharge with the consistency of pea soup will occur. When the infection spreads through the bloodstream the dog becomes excessively thirsty, and her life is in danger. Any time an unspayed female seems ill and drinks a lot of water, get her to the veterinarian immediately.

Vaginal Infection Suspect a vaginal infection whenever a female develops a discharge from her vulva; especially if the discharge occurs a week or two after her season. Painful urination also indicates the possibility of vaginal infection, as well as urinary tract infection.

GENITAL AND RELATED AREAS: MALES

The testicles in the Pomeranian do not always come down as quickly as they do in the larger breeds, but the Pom should have them by the time he reaches six months old. Before that age, don't worry if a descended testicle goes back up. In the young puppy, the testicles sometimes go up and down during times of stress or activity.

A Pom with one testicle remains fertile, but because his puppies will inherit the problem, don't use him for breeding. When both testicles fail to come down, the dog becomes sterile. A retained testicle increases the risk of cancer, so veterinarians recommend neutering if one or both of them fail to come down.

Infected testicles become inflamed, swollen and painful, causing the Pom to walk funny. If the infection is not treated immediately, the dog will become sterile.

Many male Poms get an odor-free, cream-colored discharge from the prepuce, which makes the hair gummy. This discharge is normal; however, a strong odor to the secretion indicates an infection. See Chapter 6, "Grooming Your Pomeranian," for instructions on how to keep this area clean.

HEAD INJURY

The Pomeranian, because of his small size, can easily injure his head. An object may fall on his head, a larger dog may flip him over while they're playing, or when running circles around a coffee table he can misjudge the turn, and ram headfirst into the leg. If he injures his head but doesn't lose consciousness and otherwise seems okay, put him in his crate and keep him under observation for a couple of hours. Squeeze a half-inch of Nutrical on your finger and let him lick it. However, loss of consciousness or dazed and wobbly movements mean a call to the vet.

To treat an unconscious Pom, rub a small amount of Nutrical on his upper gums, wrap him in a blanket and take him to a veterinarian. If you think he also hurt his neck, see Injuries.

HEARTWORM

The only symptom for heartworm is a cough. This doesn't even appear until after the dog has a heavy infestation, so prevention is most important in dealing with this parasite. The treatment for heartworm entails a stay at the veterinarian, then several weeks of crate rest at home. The toxic medicine used to kill the parasite poses some risk for the dog. If too many of the adult worms die at the same time, they cause blockage in the heart that can result in the death of the dog. To protect your Pomeranian, test for heartworm once a year, and keep him on preventive medication. Ask your veterinarian to give your dog a monthly heartworm preventive that also prevents adult roundworms, adult hookworms and whipworm.

HEATSTROKE

The best way to treat heatstroke is to prevent it from happening in the first place. In the summer, never leave your Pom in a car, as the interior can reach dangerous temperatures in a couple of minutes. On hot muggy days, keep your Pom in a cool shady place and always keep plenty of fresh water available.

The symptoms of heatstroke are heavy panting, deep red gums, inability to stand up, vomiting and bloody diarrhea. Without immediate treatment, the Pom will fall into a coma and die. Treat by immersing him in cool water or hosing him off, and then rush him to a veterinarian.

HEIMLICH MANEUVER
(See Choking.)

HEPATITIS

This viral disease usually occurs in young unvaccinated puppies, and they rarely survive. The disease attacks the liver and kidneys with symptoms that mimic distemper. This highly contagious disease can be prevented by vaccination.

INJURIES

Leg Fracture A leg that hangs at a crooked or odd angle suggests a broken limb. Do not try to set the bone. Treat the dog for shock, immobilize the injured leg, and take him to the veterinarian.

To **immobilize a broken leg,** make a Bobby Jones bandage. Use a strip of rolled cotton, about five to six inches wide, and wrap this around the broken leg. After you have the leg sufficiently padded, take a roll of gauze and wrap it around the cotton, covering the whole leg. To secure the bandage, wrap strips of porous adhesive tape above and below the fracture.

Before **moving an injured dog,** study the extent of his impairment. Suspect spinal cord injury if the dog cannot move his hind legs, a neck injury if he cannot move his front and back legs, and a broken leg if the limb dangles. Incorrectly moving a dog with a spinal cord injury can cause permanent damage, so you must transport him without moving his spine or neck.

Run your hands regularly over your dog to feel for any injuries.

An injured dog will be frightened and in pain, so he may snap at you; in that case muzzle him or take a folded towel and hold his head down, then slip a solid, flat board under his body. The small size of the Pomeranian makes it easy to find a usable board. In a pinch you can even use a flat baking pan or cookie sheet. Slip the flat object under the Pom and lift with one hand while holding him on with the other. It might be safer if you also tie the dog down. Wrap a gauze strip across the dog's chest area and the flat object, and tie.

If you cannot find a flat board to carry the dog and you must move him, slide one hand under the head and shoulder area and the other under the hip and torso area. Lift the dog carefully: Keeping his spine straight and flat, place him in a cardboard box and cover him with a blanket.

To move a fractured leg, immobilize the broken limb before moving the dog. If you must move him, put both hands around his rib cage and, letting the limbs hang free, pick him up.

LAMENESS

Limping   Starting at the toes, gently feel the lame leg; move the limb to its full extension, forward and back, and check the pads for cuts or burrs. If the Pom doesn't seem to be in terrible pain, and you can move the leg freely, give him some cage rest, and check the leg in an hour. Severe pain or prolonged limping suggests a problem that needs veterinarian care. (Refer to Patellar Luxation in the "Problems Particular to Pomeranians" section at the end of this chapter.)

LEPTOSPIROSIS

Infected animals, including rats, pigs, cattle and dogs spread this bacterial disease through their urine. Signs of leptospirosis include fever, anorexia, vomiting and jaundice. A viral vaccine prevents this fatal disease.

LOSS OF APPETITE

Dogs, like humans, can have an off day where they just don't feel like eating. Don't be too concerned unless the loss of appetite goes on longer than twenty-four hours. A continuing anorexia may signal an impending illness. Take the Pom's temperature; is it normal? Feel the abdomen; is it tender or rigid? Is the dog throwing up or does he have diarrhea? Any of these situations combined with a loss of appetite mean a call to the veterinarian. Consider the possibility that he is eating too many table scraps. A Pomeranian fed people food will start refusing dog food.

MOUTH

The gums in a healthy mouth look firm and pink. If you see signs of warts, white patches on the tongue or gums, bleeding or swelling, brown saliva or any ulcerations, take your dog to the veterinarian. Tartar buildup with its related gum infection causes bad breath, but regular teeth cleaning will keep his breath sweet.

To open a Pom's mouth, put a hand over his head with your fingers reaching toward his muzzle. Using your thumb and fingers, press the area before the molars. Squeeze the skin into the mouth and the dog will automatically open his jaws. With the other hand pull the lower jaw down.

MUZZLING

In an emergency you can make a muzzle with a strip of cloth. For a Pom three to six pounds, you need a strip of cloth one inch wide and a couple of feet long. A woman's cloth belt, without backing, works well. Place the cloth over the muzzle, cross the ends under the jaw, pull them to the back of the head, and tie behind the ears. It might be prudent to buy a muzzle made for the toy breeds, and add it to your first-aid kit.

Use a scarf or old hose to make a temporary muzzle, as shown

NEUTERING/SPAYING

(See Spaying/Neutering later in this chapter.)

NOSE

The normal nose feels cool, moist and dry. A hot dry nose suggests a fever; a runny nose, allergies. A fever combined with a runny nose hints at a serious problem, such as distemper. A dog with a heavily bleeding nose is in a life-threatening situation and needs immediate medical care.

Repeated frenzied sneezing, especially if the nose is runny on one side, may mean that the dog has gotten something stuck in his nostril. Do not try to remove any foreign objects by placing something, such as a cotton swab or tweezers, in the nostril. If you cannot reach the object with your fingers, call your veterinarian or instructions.

A runny nose can build into a dry thick crust. Take a soft rag, dip it in warm water and use it to soften the crust, then gently wipe the matter off the nose. After cleaning the nose, smooth on a tiny amount of petroleum jelly.

PARVOVIRUS

A highly contagious viral disease, parvovirus assaults the lymph nodes, bone marrow, heart and gastrointestinal tract. Signs of parvovirus are a high temperature, bloody diarrhea, vomiting and loss of appetite. In some forms it attacks the muscle of the heart and death occurs rapidly. Spread by the feces of

Some of the many household substances harmful to your dog.

an infected dog, the virus can come into your home via shoes and clothing. You can protect your dog from Parvo by keeping his vaccinations and booster shots up to date.

POISONING

Unless you see the dog ingest poison, it is difficult to tell when he has swallowed something toxic. Symptoms that may occur are drooling, vomiting, diarrhea, abdominal pain, staggering, slobbering, muscle tremors, bleeding gums, convulsions and, in the case of phosphorus poisoning, a garlic odor to the breath.

If these symptoms appear, call your **Poison Control Center** immediately. **1-800-548-24523** charges $30.00 per case and will only take credit card charges. **1-900-680-0000** charges $20.00 the first minute and $2.95 for each additional minute. Have the container of the poisonous substance on hand when you call the Poison Control Center, as they need the information printed on the label.

The Poison Control Center may tell you to induce vomiting. Make sure you tell them the size of your dog. If they suggest Ipecac, give one-fourth teaspoon per five pounds of body weight, or place hydrogen peroxide on the base of the tongue, at one-fourth teaspoon per five pounds of body weight. If the dog doesn't vomit within ten minutes, repeat the dose and get him to a vet.

With some poisons they may tell you to give your dog something to coat his stomach. For a mixture to coat the stomach: Mix two egg whites to one-half pint of milk, put in a drop or two of vegetable oil and feed the dog a couple of tablespoons full. If he will not drink it on his own, use the oral syringe.

Do not try to treat the dog yourself until you have spoken with the Poison Control Center or your veterinarian. The following information is offered only for your general knowledge and is not intended to replace advice from your veterinarian or Poison Control Center.

For the following poisons induce vomiting and give milk mixture: rat poisons, strychnine (unless the dog is convulsing), arsenic (you must do this early before seizures), sedatives and human medications. For fireworks, matches or phosphorus, induce vomiting but do not give the milk mixture. For antifreeze, give him the milk mixture and get him to the vet immediately.

For household cleaners such as turpentine, kerosene, gasoline, furniture polish and pine oil do not induce vomiting. Instead, feed milk and egg mixture.

For alkalis such as lye, caustic soda and caustic potash, do not induce vomiting.

For acids such as car batteries and drain cleaners, do not induce vomiting. Give milk of magnesia or Pepto-Bismol at one teaspoon per five pounds of body weight.

Other If your dog eats spoiled or rotten food, feed him the egg and milk mixture and call your veterinarian. Never feed your Pom chocolate, as it can be fatal.

Never worm your dog at the same time you treat him
with pesticides, as the combination may poison him.

Poisons also can get into your dog's system through
his skin. Immediately wash off any toxins that get on
his body. For tar, paint or grease first rub vegetable
oil on the substance before bathing the dog. If
you have trouble removing the oil, soap the oily spot
with a tiny amount of liquid dish detergent, then rinse
thoroughly.

Some common poisonous plants include poinsettia, ivy
(any kind), philodendron, chrysanthemum, lily-of-the-
valley (even the water the cut plants are placed in will
be poisonous), azalea, wisteria and daffodils.

The oak tree, its acorns and leaves, both summer and
fall, will make Pomeranians ill. My guys just love acorns
and will find them in the most hidden spots. Then they
end up with attacks of bloody diarrhea.

PORCUPINE QUILLS

Porcupine quills cause considerable pain for the
dog and he may need sedation, so you should never
attempt to remove the quills yourself. If for some
reason you find yourself in a situation where you cannot get to a veterinarian, and you must pull them yourself, give the Pom one-fourth of a baby aspirin, soften
the quills with vinegar and cut off their tips. Pull them
out with a straight, slow, steady motion. Do not remove
quills from the mouth, because the pain will be so
severe the dog must be sedated.

PULSE

Locate the pulse inside the thigh near where the
leg joins the body. When you feel the pulse, count
the number of beats per minute. The normal rate
for the Pomeranian ranges from 100 to 120 beats
per minute.

RABIES

A viral disease with an incubation period from
two weeks to several months, rabies occurs in all

warm-blooded animals, including humans. Symptoms of this fatal illness include personality changes, ferocity and delirium and paralysis of the throat. The primary mode of infection is a bite from an infected animal. Even a small house dog such as the Pomeranian can get it, so make sure you vaccinate your Pom against this horrible virus.

SHOCK

A dog in shock is not getting enough blood flow to his body, and he will act listless. At the beginning his pulse will beat fast, then, as he weakens, the beat becomes faint. His breathing appears shallow, his gums look pale and his body feels cold. Treat shock by getting him to a veterinarian, and on the way cover him with a blanket to keep him warm. Rub his body and paws to increase his circulation.

SKIN PROBLEMS

Itching   Check for fleas and if you find them treat the dog with flea shampoo and powder. Dogs can have allergies to flea bites, causing the itching to persist for up to three weeks after flea removal. Dogs develop allergies to as many substances as humans; insecticides, grass and pollen can also cause itching. Ask your veterinarian for medications to help relieve the allergic itching.

Hot spots   These are red, pus-filled, painful spots that need immediate treatment. The Pom will bite at the spot, and this chewing causes it to spread rapidly. During hot humid weather, a Pomeranian can get a hot spot from a damp undercoat, so after his bath, dry his coat thoroughly.

Calluses   Calluses are hard, thick, bare areas that appear on the dog's elbows. Giving the dog a soft bed will prevent them from forming.

Other skin problems   Circular, scaly, greasy, bald spots with an unpleasant odor; ulcers, blisters, heavy crust buildup, abscesses or bald spots with an accompanying increase in thirst are all problems that need veterinary care.

SKUNK SPRAY

Soak your dog in tomato juice, then follow with a regular bath. If tomato juice is not available, substitute lemon juice diluted with water. If the spray got into your dog's eyes, rinse them with the eyewash from your first-aid kit.

SPAYING/NEUTERING

Spaying Along with preventing pregnancy, spaying prevents pyometra and lessens the chance of mammary cancer. Veterinarians now recommend spaying before the first season. Apparently this further decreases the chance of mammary cancer. However, the Pom owner needs to weigh the risk of future mammary cancer against the immediate risk of anesthesia on a small puppy. Waiting until a Pom reaches her adult size seems the wiser choice.

Neutering The unneutered Pom will lift his leg and mark more often than a neutered dog. If you have a female in the house, the marking becomes a serious problem during her seasons. Neutering also decreases the risk of testicular cancer. Neuter the Pomeranian at around ten months of age, and make sure your veterinarian uses isoflourane. (See Anesthesia.)

ADVANTAGES OF SPAY/NEUTER

The greatest advantage of spaying (for females) or neutering (for males) your dog is that you are guaranteed your dog will not produce puppies. There are too many puppies already available for too few homes. There are other advantages as well.

ADVANTAGES OF SPAYING

No messy heats.

No "suitors" howling at your windows or waiting in your yard.

Decreased incidences of pyometra (disease of the uterus) and breast cancer.

ADVANTAGES OF NEUTERING

Lessens male aggressive and territorial behaviors, but doesn't affect the dog's personality. Behaviors are often owner-induced, so neutering is not the only answer, but it is a good start.

Prevents the need to roam in search of bitches in season.

Decreased incidences of urogenital diseases.

TEETH

You can prevent tartar buildup and tooth loss by a daily brushing. Use a toothbrush made for human infants or a cat toothbrush. Use toothpaste made especially for dogs or plain water. Never use human toothpaste, as the foaming action can cause the Pom to choke, or baking soda because of its high salt content.

The **retention of baby teeth** pops up as a common problem in the toy breeds. Some dogs get two rows of teeth in their mouth, and these puppy teeth must be extracted. The re-tained canine teeth may throw the bite off, but I have found that, unless you are plan-ning to show the dog, it is better to wait before pulling them. In many cases they eventually drop out on their own.

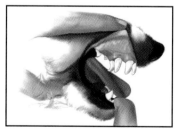

Check your Pom for retention of baby teeth.

Giving your Pomer-anian cow hooves helps in loosening up puppy teeth. I have used these hooves for years in com-plete safety, but I keep them away from my larger dogs. The powerful jaws of the bigger breeds can crack the hoof, causing splinters that lodge in the throat.

TEMPERATURE

Veterinarians take a dog's temperature while he stands, but you can take it more easily and make the dog more comfortable if you have him lie down. Put your Pom on a couch, lay him on his right side and sit next to him. Shake a rectal thermometer down until the mercury reads below 98 degrees Fahrenheit (37°C), and then put petroleum jelly on the insertion end. Lift his tail, and put the thermometer in the anus. Insert it

Check your dog's teeth frequently and brush them regularly.

85

about an inch and hold in place for three minutes. The normal temperature ranges from 100 to 102 degrees Fahrenheit.

TICKS

Ticks like to reside on the head area but can be found anywhere on the dog's body, even between the toes.

Three types of ticks (l-r): the wood tick, brown dog tick and deer tick.

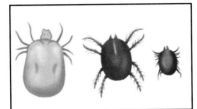

Use tweezers to remove ticks from your dog.

Squirt flea and tick spray into a small dish, dip a cotton swab into the fluid, and saturate the tick. You also can use fingernail polish remover instead of an insecticide. Wait a few minutes then use tweezers to pull out the tick. Don't jerk it out, just pull with a firm steady movement.

TUMORS

Like humans, dogs get both benign and cancerous tumors, so when grooming your dog look for any unusual lumps. You should periodically check your females in the mammary area and look for small, firm lumps near the nipples. Any mass on the dog's body should be examined by your veterinarian.

VACCINATIONS

See section on Vaccinations at beginning of chapter.

VOMITING

Vomiting is a common occurrence, but it can be a sign of more serious problems. Usually it is caused by the dog eating something indigestible such as grass, paper or garbage. Too much activity after eating also can cause him to regurgitate his meal.

Don't be concerned if the vomit looks like a yellowish foam but he doesn't act sick or have a fever; just keep a close eye on him for twenty-four hours. If he vomits a second time, give him one-half teaspoon of Pepto-Bismol. Mix moistened rice pablum with lamb or turkey baby food. Feed him this mixture in small amounts several times a day, and keep him on this diet for forty-eight hours.

TAKE A VOMITING DOG TO THE VET IF:

There is blood in the vomit.

He has a fever.

He shows signs of dehydration.

He has diarrhea along with vomiting.

The vomit looks and smells like fecal matter.

After twenty-four hours the Pom is still vomiting.

The dog becomes dehydrated.

WORMS

Tapeworms   Dogs get tapeworms by ingesting fleas. A tapeworm infestation doesn't produce any obvious symptoms, but sometimes segments of the worm will accumulate around the anal area. Fresh segments appear about one-half inch long and sometimes move. Dried segments look like rice.

Roundworms   Puppies with roundworm will not thrive, and if left untreated the condition can cause death. Puppies with an infestation will cough or gag, vomit up worms or pass them in their stool. The worm looks like a piece of spaghetti, making identification easy.

Whipworm   This worm comes by its name because it looks like a whip about two to three inches in length, with one end thicker than the other. Dogs with whipworm lose weight, have bouts of diarrhea and carry shabby coats. The difficulty of diagnosing and removing whipworms makes it essential that you put your dog on a preventive medication.

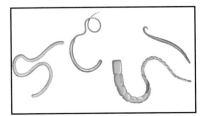

Common internal parasites (l-r): roundworm, whipworm, tapeworm and hookworm.

Hookworms Puppies with hookworm have bloody or tarry diarrhea and anemia and can quickly weaken and die. Adults with hookworm lose weight, suffer from diarrhea and develop anemia with associated weakness.

Roundworms, tapeworms and hookworms all cause disease in man, so avoid contaminating your hands with any fecal matter and keep your Pomeranians free of worms.

Problems Particular to Pomeranians

Like any other breed, the Pomeranian encounters certain health conditions more than others. Some Pomeranians will retain their puppy teeth, some will go lame or develop thyroid problems, and others will go bald. Except for the baldness, most of these problems can be corrected. I am listing these conditions because they appear in the breed, but don't become overly concerned, as the majority of Pomeranians don't experience them and remain healthy and hardy throughout their lives. The information on **patellar luxation** and **black skin disease** can be useful in helping you choose a puppy.

ANESTHESIA

The Pomeranian, like other toy breeds, doesn't tolerate anesthesia very well, especially when more than one procedure is performed. Isoflourane, a relatively new anesthetic, works safely on the Pom and most veterinarians are now using it. For some reason, most deaths of Pomeranians while under anesthesia seem to happen when the vet performs two procedures at the same time: such as spaying and teeth cleaning.

BLACK SKIN AND BALDNESS

Several health problems, such as Cushings disease, hypothyroidism, cortisone excess and estrogen deficiency cause bald areas of dark grey skin. But in the Pomeranian breed, the most common cause of these symptoms is what the Pomeranian fancy calls "Black Skin Disease." Some also call it elephant skin disease, the Pom disease or simply the Skin Disease.

Veterinarians diagnose it as adult growth hormone disorder. However, a research project in Tennessee discovered that normal-coated Poms also tested low on the growth hormone. This same research project found that, while the condition seems to run in certain families, there was no clear evidence of an inheritance factor. I'm not a vet or a research scientist, but from my own and other breeders' experiences I have come to believe that it is an inherited condition. Before buying a Pomeranian ask the breeder if any of the puppies' ancestors had the black skin disease. Also ask if any older puppies from the sire and dam of your prospective pup have come down with this condition.

Signs of black skin disease do not appear right away. At six months

WHEN TO CALL THE VET

In any emergency situation, you should call your veterinarian immediately. You can make the difference in your dog's life by staying as calm as possible when you call and by giving the doctor or the assistant as much information as possible before you leave for the clinic. That way, the vet will be able to take immediate, specific action to remedy your dog's situation.

Emergencies include acute abdominal pain, suspected poisoning, snakebite, burns, frostbite, shock, dehydration, abnormal vomiting or bleeding, and deep wounds. You are the best judge of your dog's health, as you live with and observe him every day. Don't hesitate to call your veterinarian if you suspect trouble.

Pomeranian puppies start growing their adult coat. With black skin disease, the puppy retains the juvenile coat and he never gets an adult coat. At about eighteen months old the puppy coat starts falling

89

out and he goes bald. In some cases, the puppy will get the adult coat and go bald later. These Poms usually do not lose as much hair as the ones who never grew adult fur.

As the dog develops bald patches, his skin turns a dark grey color. It may remain smooth or get a little rough, but it doesn't develop any open sores or an offensive odor. The condition appears more often in males. The tail, rump and backs of thighs go bald. Some dogs lose all their belly hair and others go completely bald except for the legs and head. Otherwise, the dog remains healthy.

An Elizabethan collar keeps your dog from licking a fresh wound.

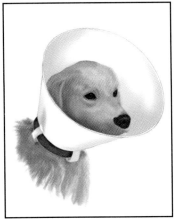

No cure for this condition exists, but sometimes the coat can be made to grow again. Often, neutering the male brings back the coat, but this doesn't work for every Pom. To further confuse the issue, the coat sometimes comes back when the Pom reaches seven years old. Hormone replacement shots can induce coat growth, but they are expensive and may cause the dog to develop diabetes.

Treatment for a suspected case   Any Pom puppy over six months of age who hasn't gotten his adult coat should be bathed several times a month with a tar-and-sulfur shampoo. Many times this will delay the onset of hair loss.

For a Pom who has already started getting bald, you must rule out all diseases that cause hair loss. Ask your vet to test for thyroid disease and to check for fungus or mites. You may want to discuss with him the safety of hormone replacement therapy, and get his opinion of the sulfur treatment (described below).

For the dog that has already gone bald, the Pomeranian fancy uses a common, but unscientific, oil-and-sulfur application to treat the condition. I used this treatment on two of my dogs, brought back both of their coats, and managed to keep one in full coat for over three years.

Obtain Flowers of Sulfur, a nonprescription item, from your drugstore. If your pharmacist doesn't carry it, ask him to order it for you. Most bottles of sulfur carry a printed recipe for an ointment, but if you can't find one, here it is: Mix one part sulfur with six parts fresh lard. Blend until smooth and creamy with a uniform yellow color.

To treat your Pom, give him a bath with tar-and-sulfur shampoo, leave it on for five minutes, then rinse. Dry the coat, then apply the ointment to the bald spots. The skin absorbs most of the ointment, but some may stick on the fur near the coated area. Once a week, between baths, apply more ointment. Repeat this routine faithfully every seven days until his hair starts growing. It is important to bathe the dog after a week, because the ointment that sticks in the fur may accumulate dirt and cause a skin infection. New hair should start growing in the bald spots in about four weeks. After the new hair gets so long you can't apply the sulfur ointment, bathe the dog with the tar-and-sulfur shampoo once or twice a month.

If you want to try this treatment, be aware that it isn't based on scientific evidence. Discuss it with your veterinarian first.

Finally, if you wish, call the AKC and obtain the telephone number of the secretary of the American Pomeranian Club. Ask

IDENTIFYING YOUR DOG

It's a terrible thing to think about, but your dog could somehow, someday, get lost or stolen. How would you get him back? Your best bet would be to have some form of identification on your dog. You can choose from a collar and tags, a tattoo, a microchip or a combination of these three.

Every dog should wear a buckle collar with identification tags. They are the quickest and easiest way for a stranger to identify your dog. It's best to inscribe the tags with your name and phone number; you don't need to include your dog's name.

There are two ways to permanently identify your dog. The first is a tattoo, placed on the inside of your dog's thigh. The tattoo should be your social security number or your dog's AKC registration number.

The second is a microchip, a rice-sized pellet that's inserted under the dog's skin at the base of the neck, between the shoulder blades. When a scanner is passed over the dog, it will beep, notifying the person that the dog has a chip. The scanner will then show a code, identifying the dog. Microchips are becoming more and more popular and are certainly the wave of the future.

the secretary if the Committee on Skin Diseases still exists, and if so, to refer you to the chairman. Hopefully the committee chairman will be able to advise you of the latest information he or she may have on black skin disease. In the meantime remember that a Pomeranian with this condition lives a normal life, except he may need to wear a sweater during the winter, and otherwise remains a healthy, wonderful, loving pet.

HYPOGLYCEMIA

This sudden drop in blood sugar occurs more often in the toy breeds. It usually happens to very young puppies, but in severely stressful situations it also can affect an adult Pomeranian. Heavy activity, the stress of a new home, stomach upsets, head injuries and severe pain can cause the condition. The symptoms entail sudden collapse, weakness, tremors and sometimes convulsions. If left untreated it can lead to coma and death. Rub a one-eighth-inch bead of Nutrical on the gums of any puppy that displays symptoms of hypoglycemia.

In a stressful situation, protect your new puppy by putting corn syrup in his drinking water: one-half teaspoon to four ounces of water. Use this sweetened water for the first three days after he moves into your home. Too much added sweetening in the diet can cause the blood sugar to swing widely, thus bringing on the very problem you're trying to prevent, so only use the Karo syrup for the first few days.

For prevention in an adult Pomeranian, feed a good-quality dog food and keep Nutrical in the house. When baby teeth are pulled, or your dog undergoes any type of surgery, such as spaying or neutering, give him some Nutrical as soon as he gets home. If he is able to drink, give him some water at the same time. Anytime a dog becomes unconscious, rub Nutrical on his gums.

HYPOTHYROIDISM

Loss of hair from the dog's back and thighs, along with sluggishness, weight gain, scaling skin and intolerance to cold indicates hypothyroidism, though sometimes a distinct change in personality is the only symptom. Your veterinarian can diagnose this treatable condition with a blood test.

PATELLAR LUXATION

A condition in which the kneecap slips out of its groove, luxation is common in the toy breeds. It is usually an inherited disorder but also can be caused by an injury. The degree of luxation varies from a mild case that barely affects the dog to a severe one that requires surgery.

A Pom who receives regular veterinary checkups and good care at home will reward her owner with many healthy years.

Don't let a diagnosis of patellar luxation discourage you. The majority of Pomeranians with this condition live normal lives, and if your puppy's luxation is severe, surgery will take care of the problem. My first Pomeranian, Shadow, popped her left knee out twice, then lived to eleven without further incident.

Signs of Luxation In mild cases the foot on the affected leg toes in, and the hock points out. When the knee pops out, the dog will stretch his rear leg along his side, with his paw pointing toward his nose, and he will experience considerable pain. Take your dog to the veterinarian and ask her to teach you how to put the knee back in place. Please note that a Pom with patellar luxation should not be bred.

93

Euthanasia

As your Pomeranian ages, there are many things you can do to help him be more comfortable, but there will come a time when you realize he is suffering more than he needs to. The decision about when to euthanize your dog is a very personal one; consult your veterinarian, but don't make her decide for you. You live with your dog day in, day out and know him best.

When the time comes, go with your dog to the vet's and stay with him while the vet injects an overdose of anesthetic. Your dog will ease into sleep, comforted by you, and the last thing he'll remember is your love.

Your Happy, Healthy Pet

Your Dog's Name _____

Name on Your Dog's Pedigree (if your dog has one) _____

_____

Where Your Dog Came From _____

_____

Your Dog's Birthday _____

Your Dog's Veterinarian

    Name _____

    Address _____

    Phone Number _____

    Emergency Number _____

Your Dog's Health

    Vaccines

    type _____ date given _____

    type _____ date given _____

    type _____ date given _____

    type _____ date given _____

    Heartworm

    date tested _____ type used_____ start date _____

Your Dog's License Number _____

Groomer's Name and Number _____

Dogsitter/Walker's Name and Number _____

Awards Your Dog Has Won

    Award _____ date earned _____

    Award _____ date earned _____

part three

Enjoying
your
Dog

chapter 8

Basic
Training

by Ian Dunbar, Ph.D., MRCVS

Training is the jewel in the crown—the most important aspect of doggy husbandry. There is no more important variable influencing dog behavior and temperament than the dog's education: A well-trained, well-behaved and good-natured puppydog is always a joy to live with, but an untrained and uncivilized dog can be a perpetual nightmare. Moreover, deny the dog an education and it will not have the opportunity to fulfill its own canine potential; neither will it have the ability to communicate effectively with its human companions.

Luckily, modern psychological training methods are easy, efficient and effective and, above all, considerably dog-friendly and user-friendly. Doggy education is as simple as it is enjoyable. But before you can have a good time play-training with your new dog, you have to learn what to do and how to do it. There is no bigger variable influencing the success of dog training than the *owner's* experience and expertise. *Before you embark on the dog's education, you must first educate yourself.*

Basic Training for Owners

Ideally, basic owner training should begin well *before* you select your dog. Find out all you can about your chosen breed first, then master rudimentary training and handling skills. If you already have your puppy/dog, owner training is a dire emergency—the clock is running! Especially for puppies, the first few weeks at home are the most important and influential days in the dog's life. Indeed, the cause of most adolescent and adult problems may be traced back to the initial days the pup explores his new home. This is the time to establish the *status quo*—to teach the puppy/dog how you would like him to behave and so prevent otherwise quite predictable problems.

In addition to consulting breeders and breed books such as this one (which understandably have a positive breed bias), seek out as many pet owners with your breed you can find. Good points are obvious. What you want to find out are the breed-specific *problems*, so you can nip them in the bud. In particular, you should talk to owners with *adolescent* dogs and make a list of all anticipated problems. Most important, *test drive* at least half a dozen adolescent and adult dogs of your breed yourself. An eight-week-old puppy is deceptively easy to handle, but she will acquire adult size, speed and strength in just four months, so you should learn now what to prepare for.

Puppy and pet dog training classes offer a convenient venue to locate pet owners and observe dogs in action. For a list of suitable trainers in your area, contact the Association of Pet Dog Trainers (see Chapter 13). You may also begin your basic owner training by observing other owners in class. Watch as many classes and test drive as many dogs as possible. Select an upbeat, dog-friendly, people-friendly, fun-and-games, puppydog pet training class to learn the ropes. Also, watch training videos and read training books (see Chapter 12). You must find out what to do and how to do it *before* you have to do it.

Principles of Training

Most people think training comprises teaching the dog to do things such as sit, speak and roll over, but even a four-week-old pup knows how to do these things already. Instead, the first step in training involves teaching the dog human words for each dog behavior and activity and for each aspect of the dog's environment. That way you, the owner, can more easily participate in the dog's domestic education by directing him to perform specific actions appropriately, that is, at the right time, in the right place, and so on. Training opens communication channels, enabling an educated dog to at least understand the owner's requests.

In addition to teaching a dog *what* we want her to do, it is also necessary to teach her *why* she should do what we ask. Indeed, 95 percent of training revolves around motivating the dog *to want to do* what we want. Dogs often understand what their owners want; they just don't see the point of doing it—especially when the owner's repetitively boring and seemingly senseless instructions are totally at odds with much more pressing and exciting doggy distractions. It is not so much the dog who is being stubborn or dominant; rather, it is the owner who has failed to acknowledge the dog's needs and feelings and to approach training from the dog's point of view.

The Meaning of Instructions

The secret to successful training is learning how to use training lures to predict or prompt specific behaviors—to coax the dog to do what you want *when* you want. Any highly valued object (such as a treat or toy) may be used as a lure, which the dog will follow with his eyes and nose. Moving the lure in specific ways entices the dog to move his nose, head and entire body in specific ways. In fact, by learning the art of manipulating various lures, it is possible to teach the dog to assume virtually any body position and perform any action. Once you have control over the expression of the dog's behaviors and can elicit any body position or behavior at will, you can easily teach the dog to perform on request.

Tell your dog what you want him to do, use a lure to entice him to respond correctly, then profusely praise

Teach your dog words for each activity he needs to know, like down.

and maybe reward him once he performs the desired action. For example, verbally request "Fido, sit!" while you move a squeaky toy upwards and backwards over the dog's muzzle (lure-movement and hand signal), smile knowingly as he looks up (to follow the lure) and sits down (as a result of canine anatomical engineering), then praise him to distraction ("Goood Fido!"). Squeak the toy, offer a training treat and give your dog and yourself a pat on the back.

Being able to elicit desired responses over and over enables the owner to reward the dog over and over. Consequently, the dog begins to think training is fun. For example, the more the dog is rewarded for sitting, the more she enjoys sitting. Eventually the dog comes to realize that, whereas most sitting is appreciated, sitting immediately upon request usually prompts especially enthusiastic praise and a slew of high-level rewards. The dog begins to sit on cue much of the time, showing that she is starting to grasp the meaning of the owner's verbal request and hand signal.

Why Comply?

Most dogs enjoy initial lure/reward training and are only too happy to comply with their owners' wishes. Unfortunately, repetitive drilling without appreciative feedback tends to diminish the dog's enthusiasm until he eventually fails to see the point of complying anymore. Moreover, as the dog approaches adolescence he becomes more easily distracted as he develops other interests. Lengthy sessions with repetitive exercises tend to bore and demotivate both parties. If it's not fun, the owner doesn't do it and neither does the dog.

Integrate training into your dog's life: The greater number of training sessions each day and the *shorter* they are, the more willingly compliant your dog will become. Make sure to have a short (just a few seconds) training interlude before every enjoyable canine activity. For example, ask your dog to sit to greet people, to sit before you throw his Frisbee, and to sit for his supper. Really, sitting is no different from a canine "please." Also, include numerous short training interludes during every enjoyable canine pastime, for example, when playing with the dog or when he is running in the park. In this fashion, doggy distractions may be effectively converted into rewards for training. Just as all games have rules, fun becomes training . . . and training becomes fun.

Eventually, rewards actually become unnecessary to continue motivating your dog. If trained with consideration and kindness, performing the desired behaviors will become self-rewarding and, in a sense, your dog will motivate himself. Just as it is not necessary to reward a human companion during an enjoyable walk in the park, or following a game of tennis, it is hardly necessary to reward our best friend—the dog—for walking by our side or while playing fetch. Human company during enjoyable activities is reward enough for most dogs.

Even though your dog has become self-motivating, it's still good to praise and pet him a lot and offer rewards once in a while, especially for a good job well done. And if for no other reason, praising and rewarding others is good for the human heart.

To train your dog, you need gentle hands, a loving heart and a good attitude.

Punishment

Without a doubt, lure/reward training is by far the best way to teach: Entice your dog to do what you want and then reward him for doing so. Unfortunately, a human shortcoming is to take the good for granted and to moan and groan at the bad. Specifically, the dog's many good behaviors are ignored while the owner focuses on punishing the dog for making mistakes. In extreme cases, instruction is *limited* to punishing mistakes made by a trainee dog, child, employee or husband, even though it has been proven punishment training is notoriously inefficient and ineffective and is decidedly unfriendly and combative. It teaches the dog that training is a drag, almost as quickly as it teaches the dog to dislike his trainer. Why treat our best friends like our worst enemies?

Punishment training is also much more laborious and time consuming. Whereas it takes only a finite amount of time to teach a dog what to chew, for example, it takes much, much longer to punish the dog for each and every mistake. Remember, *there is only one right way!* So why not teach that right way from the outset?!

To make matters worse, punishment training causes severe lapses in the dog's reliability. Since it is obviously impossible to punish the dog each and every time she misbehaves, the dog quickly learns to distinguish between those times when she must comply (so as to avoid impending punishment) and those times when she need not comply, because punishment is impossible. Such times include when the dog is off leash and only six feet away, when the owner is otherwise engaged (talking to a friend, watching television, taking a shower, tending to the baby or chatting on the telephone), or when the dog is left at home alone.

Instances of misbehavior will be numerous when the owner is away, because even when the dog complied in the owner's looming presence, he did so unwillingly. The dog was forced to act against his will, rather than moulding his will to want to please. Hence, when the owner is absent, not only does the dog know he need not comply, he simply does not want to. Again, the trainee is not a stubborn vindictive beast, but rather the trainer has failed to teach.

Punishment training invariably creates unpredictable Jekyll and Hyde behavior.

Trainer's Tools

Many training books extol the virtues of a vast array of training paraphernalia and electronic and metallic gizmos, most of which are designed for canine restraint, correction and punishment, rather than for actual facilitation of doggy education. In reality, most effective training tools are not found in stores; they come from within ourselves. In addition to a willing dog, all you really need is a functional human brain, gentle hands, a loving heart and a good attitude.

In terms of equipment, all dogs do require a quality buckle collar to sport dog tags and to attach the leash (for safety and to comply with local leash laws). Hollow chewtoys (like Kongs or sterilized longbones) and a dog bed or collapsible crate are a must for housetraining. Three additional tools are required:

1. specific lures (training treats and toys) to predict and prompt specific desired behaviors;

2. rewards (praise, affection, training treats and toys) to reinforce for the dog what a lot of fun it all is; and

3. knowledge—how to convert the dog's favorite activities and games (potential distractions to training) into "life-rewards," which may be employed to facilitate training.

The most powerful of these is *knowledge*. Education is the key! Watch training classes, participate in training classes, watch videos, read books, enjoy playtraining with your dog, and then your dog will say "Please," and your dog will say "Thank you!"

Housetraining

If dogs were left to their own devices, certainly they would chew, dig and bark for entertainment and then no doubt highlight a few areas of their living space with sprinkles of urine, in much the same way we decorate by hanging pictures. Consequently, when we ask a dog to live with us, we must teach him *where* he may dig and perform his toilet duties, *what* he may chew and *when* he may bark. After all, when left at home alone for many hours, we cannot expect the dog to amuse himself by completing crosswords or watching the soaps on TV!

Also, it would be decidedly unfair to keep the house rules a secret from the dog, and then get angry and punish the poor critter for inevitably transgressing rules he did not even know existed. Remember, without adequate education and guidance, the dog will be forced to establish his own rules—doggy rules—that most probably will be at odds with the owner's view of domestic living.

Since most problems develop during the first few days the dog is at home, prospective dog owners must be certain they are quite clear about the principles of housetraining *before* they get a dog. Early misbehaviors quickly become established as the status quo—

becoming firmly entrenched as hard-to-break bad habits, which set the precedent for years to come. Make sure to teach your dog good habits right from the start. Good habits are just as hard to break as bad ones!

Ideally, when a new dog comes home, try to arrange for someone to be present for as much as possible during the first few days (for adult dogs) or weeks for puppies. With only a little forethought, it is surprisingly easy to find a puppy sitter, such as a retired person, who would be willing to eat from your refrigerator and watch your television while keeping an eye on the newcomer to encourage the dog to play with chewtoys and to ensure he goes outside on a regular basis.

POTTY TRAINING

To teach the dog where to relieve himself:

1. never let him make a single mistake;
2. let him know where you want him to go; and
3. handsomely reward him for doing so: "GOOOOOOOD DOG!!!" liver treat, liver treat, liver treat!

PREVENTING MISTAKES

A single mistake is a training disaster, since it heralds many more in future weeks. And each time the dog soils the house, this further reinforces the dog's unfortunate preference for an indoor, carpeted toilet. *Do not let an unhousetrained dog have full run of the house if you are away from home or cannot pay full attention.* Instead, confine the dog to an area where elimination is appropriate, such as an outdoor run or, better still, a small, comfortable indoor kennel with access to an outdoor run. When confined in this manner, most dogs will naturally housetrain themselves.

If that's not possible, confine the dog to an area, such as a utility room, kitchen, basement or garage, where elimination may not be desired in the long run but as an interim measure it is certainly preferable to doing it all around the house. Use newspaper to cover the floor of the dog's day room. The newspaper may be used to soak up the urine and to wrap up and dispose of the feces. Once your dog develops a preferred spot for eliminating, it is only necessary to cover that part of the floor with newspaper. The smaller papered area may then be moved (only a little each day) towards the door to the outside. Thus the dog will develop the tendency to go to the door when he needs to relieve himself.

The first few weeks at home are the most important and influential in your dog's life.

Never confine an unhousetrained dog to a crate for long periods. Doing so would force the dog to soil the crate and ruin its usefulness as an aid for housetraining (see the following discussion).

TEACHING WHERE

In order to teach your dog where you would like her to do her business, you have to be there to direct the proceedings—an obvious, yet often neglected, fact of life. In order to be there to teach the dog *where* to go, you need to know *when* she needs to go. Indeed, the success of housetraining depends on the owner's ability to predict these times. Certainly, a regular feeding schedule will facilitate prediction somewhat, but there is

nothing like "loading the deck" and influencing the timing of the outcome yourself!

Whenever you are at home, make sure the dog is under constant supervision and/or confined to a small area. If already well trained, simply instruct the dog to lie down in his bed or basket. Alternatively, confine the dog to a crate (doggy den) or tie-down (a short, 18-inch lead that can be clipped to an eye hook in the baseboard). Short-term close confinement strongly inhibits urination and defecation, since the dog does not want to soil his sleeping area. Thus, when you release the puppydog each hour, he will definitely need to urinate immediately and defecate every third or fourth hour. Keep the dog confined to his doggy den and take him to his intended toilet area each hour, every hour, and on the hour.

When taking your dog outside, instruct him to sit quietly before opening the door—he will soon learn to sit by the door when he needs to go out!

TEACHING WHY

Being able to predict when the dog needs to go enables the owner to be on the spot to praise and reward the dog. Each hour, hurry the dog to the intended toilet area in the yard, issue the appropriate instruction ("Go pee!" or "Go poop!"), then give the dog three to four minutes to produce. Praise and offer a couple of training treats when successful. The treats are important because many people fail to praise their dogs with feeling . . . and housetraining is hardly the time for understatement. So either loosen up and enthusiastically praise that dog: "Wuzzzer-wuzzer-wuzzer, hoooser good wuffer den? Hoooo went pee for Daddy?" Or say "Good dog!" as best you can and offer the treats for effect.

Following elimination is an ideal time for a spot of playtraining in the yard or house. Also, an empty dog may be allowed greater freedom around the house for the next half hour or so, just as long as you keep an eye out to make sure he does not get into other kinds of mischief. If you are preoccupied and cannot pay full attention, confine the dog to his doggy den once more to enjoy a peaceful snooze or to play with his many chewtoys.

If your dog does not eliminate within the allotted time outside—no biggie! Back to his doggy den, and then try again after another hour.

As I own large dogs, I always feel more relaxed walking an empty dog, knowing that I will not need to finish our stroll weighted down with bags of feces! Beware of falling into the trap of walking the dog to get it to eliminate. The good ol' dog walk is such an enormous highlight in the dog's life that it represents the single biggest potential reward in domestic dogdom. However, when in a hurry, or during inclement weather, many owners abruptly terminate the walk the moment the dog has done its business. This, in effect, severely punishes the dog for doing the right thing, in the right place at the right time. Consequently, many dogs become strongly inhibited from eliminating outdoors because they know it will signal an abrupt end to an otherwise thoroughly enjoyable walk.

Instead, instruct the dog to relieve himself in the yard prior to going for a walk. If you follow the above instructions, most dogs soon learn to eliminate on cue. As soon as the dog eliminates, praise (and offer a treat or two)—"Good dog! Let's go walkies!" Use the walk as a reward for eliminating in the yard. If the dog does not go, put him back in his doggy den and think about a walk later on. You will find with a "No feces–no walk" policy, your dog will become one of the fastest defecators in the business.

If you do not have a back yard, instruct the dog to eliminate right outside your front door prior to the walk. Not only will this facilitate clean up and disposal of the feces in your own trash can but, also, the walk may again be used as a colossal reward.

CHEWING AND BARKING

Short-term close confinement also teaches the dog that occasional quiet moments are a reality of domestic living. Your puppydog is extremely impressionable during his first few weeks at home. Regular confinement at this time soon exerts a calming influence over the dog's personality. Remember, once the dog is housetrained and calmer, there will be a whole lifetime ahead for the dog to enjoy full run of the house and garden. On the other hand, by letting the newcomer have unrestricted access to the entire household and allowing him to run willy-nilly, he will most certainly develop a bunch of behavior problems in short order, no doubt necessitating confinement later in life. It would not be fair to remedially restrain and confine a dog you have trained, through neglect, to run free.

When confining the dog, make sure he always has an impressive array of suitable chewtoys. Kongs and sterilized longbones (both readily available from pet stores) make the best chewtoys, since they are hollow and may be stuffed with treats to heighten the dog's interest. For example, by stuffing the little hole at the top of a Kong with a small piece of freeze-dried liver, the dog will not want to leave it alone.

Remember, treats do not have to be junk food and they certainly should not represent extra calories. Rather, treats should be part of each dog's regular daily diet:

Make sure your puppy has suitable chewtoys.

Some food may be served in the dog's bowl for breakfast and dinner, some food may be used as training treats, and some food may be used for stuffing chewtoys. I regularly stuff my dogs' many Kongs with different shaped biscuits and kibble. The kibble seems to fall out fairly easily, as do the oval-shaped biscuits, thus rewarding the dog instantaneously for checking out the chewtoys. The bone-shaped biscuits fall out after a while, rewarding the dog for worrying at the chewtoy. But the triangular biscuits never come out. They remain inside the Kong as lures, maintaining the dog's fascination with its chewtoy. To further focus the dog's interest, I always make sure to flavor the triangular biscuits by rubbing them with a little cheese or freeze-dried liver.

If stuffed chewtoys are reserved especially for times the dog is confined, the puppy-dog will soon learn to enjoy quiet moments in her doggy den and she will quickly develop a chewtoy habit—a good habit! This is a simple *passive training* process; all the owner has to do is set up the situation and the dog all but trains herself—easy and effective. Even when the dog is given run of the house, her first inclination will be to indulge her rewarding chewtoy habit rather than destroying less-attractive household articles, such as curtains, carpets, chairs and compact disks. Similarly, a chewtoy chewer will be less inclined to scratch and chew herself excessively. Also, if the dog busies herself as a recreational chewer, she will be less inclined to develop into a recreational barker or digger when left at home alone.

Stuff a number of chewtoys whenever the dog is left confined and remove the extra-special-tasting treats when you return. Your dog will now amuse himself with his chewtoys before falling asleep and then resume playing with his chewtoys when he expects you to return. Since most owner-absent misbehavior happens right after you leave and right before your expected return, your puppydog will now be conveniently preoccupied with his chewtoys at these times.

Come and Sit

Most puppies will happily approach virtually anyone, whether called or not; that is, until they collide with

To teach come, call your dog, open your arms as a welcoming signal, wave a toy or a treat and praise for every step in your direction.

adolescence and develop other more important doggy interests, such as sniffing a multiplicity of exquisite odors on the grass. Your mission, Mr. and/or Ms. Owner, is to teach and reward the pup for coming reliably, willingly and happily when called—and you have just three months to get it done. Unless adequately reinforced, your puppy's tendency to approach people will self-destruct by adolescence.

Call your dog ("Fido, come!"), open your arms (and maybe squat down) as a welcoming signal, waggle a treat or toy as a lure, and reward the puppydog when he comes running. Do not wait to praise the dog until he reaches you—he may come 95 percent of the way and then run off after some distraction. Instead, praise the dog's *first* step towards you and continue praising enthusiastically for *every* step he takes in your direction.

When the rapidly approaching puppy dog is three lengths away from impact, instruct him to sit ("Fido, sit!") and hold the lure in front of you in an outstretched hand to prevent him from hitting you mid-chest and knocking you flat on your back! As Fido decelerates to nose the lure, move the treat upwards and backwards just over his muzzle with an upwards motion of your extended arm (palm-upwards). As the dog looks up to follow the lure, he will sit down (if he jumps up, you are holding the lure too high). Praise the dog for sitting. Move backwards and call him again. Repeat this many times over, always praising when Fido comes and sits; on occasion, reward him.

For the first couple of trials, use a training treat both as a lure to entice the dog to come and sit and as a reward for doing so. Thereafter, try to use different items as lures and rewards. For example, lure the dog with a Kong or Frisbee but reward her with a food treat. Or lure the dog with a food treat but pat her and throw a tennis ball as a reward. After just a few repetitions, dispense with the lures and rewards; the dog will begin to respond willingly to your verbal requests and hand signals just for the prospect of praise from your heart and affection from your hands.

Instruct every family member, friend and visitor how to get the dog to come and sit. Invite people over for a series of pooch parties; do not keep the pup a secret— let other people enjoy this puppy, and let the pup enjoy other people. Puppydog parties are not only fun, they easily attract a lot of people to help *you* train *your* dog. Unless you teach your dog *how* to meet people, that is, to sit for greetings, no doubt the dog will resort to jumping up. Then you and the visitors will get annoyed, and the dog will be punished. This is not fair. *Send out those invitations for puppy parties and teach your dog to be mannerly and socially acceptable.*

Even though your dog quickly masters obedient recalls in the house, his reliability may falter when playing in the back yard or local park. Ironically, it is *the owner* who has unintentionally trained the dog *not* to respond in these instances. By allowing the dog to play and run around and otherwise have a good time, but then to call the dog to put him on leash to take him home, the dog quickly learns playing is fun but training is a drag. Thus, playing in the park becomes a severe distraction, which works against training. Bad news!

Instead, whether playing with the dog off leash or on leash, request him to come at frequent intervals— say, every minute or so. On most occasions, praise and pet the dog for a few seconds while he is sitting, then tell him to go play again. For especially fast recalls, offer a couple of training treats and take the time to praise and pet the dog enthusiastically before releasing him. The dog will learn that coming when called is not necessarily the end of the play session, and neither is it the end of the world; rather, it signals an enjoyable, quality time-out with the owner before resuming play once more. In fact, playing in the park now becomes a very effective life-reward, which works to facilitate training by reinforcing each obedient and timely recall. Good news!

Sit, Down, Stand and Rollover

Teaching the dog a variety of body positions is easy for owner and dog, impressive for spectators and extremely useful for all. Using lure-reward techniques, it is possible to train several positions at once to verbal commands or hand signals (which impress the socks off onlookers).

Sit and ~~*down*~~—the two control commands—prevent or resolve nearly a hundred behavior problems. For example, if the dog happily and obediently sits or lies down when requested, he cannot jump on visitors, dash out the front door, run around and chase its tail, pester other dogs, harass cats or annoy family, friends or strangers. Additionally, "sit" or "down" are better emergency commands for off-leash control.

It is easier to teach and maintain a reliable sit than maintain a reliable recall. *Sit* is the purest and simplest of commands—either the dog is sitting or he is not. If there is any change of circumstances or potential danger in the park, for example, simply instruct the dog to sit. If he sits, you have a number of options: allow the dog to resume playing when he is safe; walk up and put the dog on leash, or call the dog. The dog will be much more likely to come when called if he has already acknowledged his compliance by sitting. If the dog does not sit in the park—train him to!

Stand and *rollover-stay* are the two positions for examining the dog. Your veterinarian will love you to distraction if you take a little time to teach the dog to stand still and roll over and play possum. Also, your vet bills will be smaller. The rollover-stay is an especially useful command and is really just a variation of the down-stay: whereas the dog lies prone in the traditional down, she lies supine in the rollover-stay.

As with teaching come and sit, the training techniques to teach the dog to assume all other body positions on cue are user-friendly and dog-friendly. Simply give the appropriate request, lure the dog into the desired body position using a training treat or toy and then *praise* (and maybe reward) the dog as soon as he complies. Try not to touch the dog to get him to respond. If you teach the dog by guiding him into position, the dog will quickly learn that rump-pressure means sit, for example, but as yet you still have no control over your dog if he is just six feet away. It will still be necessary to teach the dog to sit on request. So do not make training a time-consuming two-step process; instead, teach the dog to sit to a verbal request or hand signal from the outset. Once the dog sits willingly when requested, by all means use your hands to pet the dog when he does so.

To teach **down** when the dog is already sitting, say "Fido, down!," hold the lure in one hand (palm down) and lower that hand to the floor between the dog's forepaws. As the dog lowers his head to follow the lure, slowly move the lure away from the dog just a fraction (in front of his paws). The dog will lie down as he stretches his nose forward to follow the lure. Praise the dog when he does so. If the dog stands up, you pulled the lure away too far and too quickly.

When teaching the dog to lie down from the standing position, say "down" and lower the lure to the floor as before. Once the dog has lowered his forequarters and assumed a play bow, gently and slowly move the lure *towards* the dog between his forelegs. Praise the dog as soon as his rear end plops down.

After just a couple of trials it will be possible to alternate sits and downs and have the dog energetically perform doggy push-ups. Praise the dog a lot, and after half a dozen or so push-ups reward the dog with a training treat or toy. You will notice the more energetically you move your arm—upwards (palm up) to get the dog to sit, and downwards (palm down) to get the dog to lie down—the more energetically the dog responds to your requests. Now try training the dog in silence and you will notice he has also learned to respond to hand signals. Yeah! Not too shabby for the first session.

To teach **stand** from the sitting position, say "Fido, stand," slowly move the lure half a dog-length away from the dog's nose, keeping it at nose level, and praise the dog as he stands to follow the lure. As soon

Using a food lure to teach sit, down and stand. 1) "Phoenix, Sit." 2) Hand palm upwards, move h[...] up and back over dog's muzzle. 3) "Good sit, Phoenix!" 4) "Phoenix, down." 5) Hand palm downwards, move lure down to lie between dog's forepaws. 6) "Phoenix, off. Good down, Phoenix!" 7) "Phoe[...] sit!" 8) Palm upwards, move lure up and back, keeping it close to dog's muzzle. 9) "Good sit, Phoeni[...]

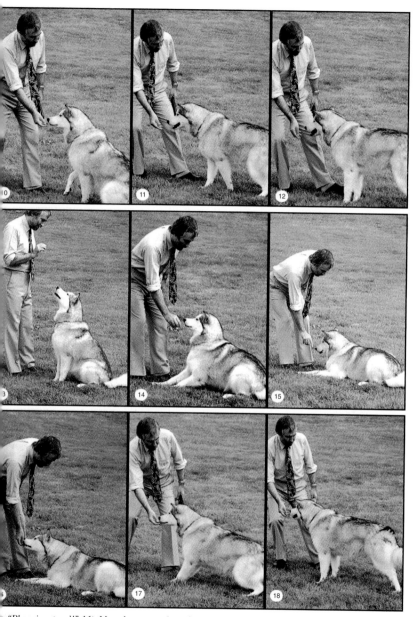

"Phoenix, stand!" 11) Move lure away from dog at nose height, then lower it a tad. 12) "Phoenix, Good stand, Phoenix!" 13) "Phoenix, down!" 14) Hand palm downwards, move lure down to lie ween dog's forepaws. 15) "Phoenix, off! Good down-stay, Phoenix!" 16) "Phoenix, stand!" 17) Move e away from dog's muzzle up to nose height. 18) "Phoenix, off! Good stand-stay, Phoenix. Now we'll ke the vet and groomer happy!"

as the dog stands, lower the lure to just beneath the dog's chin to entice him to look down; otherwise he will stand and then sit immediately. To prompt the dog to stand from the down position, move the lure half a dog-length upwards and away from the dog, holding the lure at standing nose height from the floor.

Teaching *rollover* is best started from the down position, with the dog lying on one side, or at least with both hind legs stretched out on the same side. Say "Fido, bang!" and move the lure backwards and alongside the dog's muzzle to its elbow (on the side of its outstretched hind legs). Once the dog looks to the side and backwards, very slowly move the lure upwards to the dog's shoulder and backbone. Tickling the dog in the goolies (groin area) often invokes a reflex-raising of the hind leg as an appeasement gesture, which facilitates the tendency to roll over. If you move the lure too quickly and the dog jumps into the standing position, have patience and start again. As soon as the dog rolls onto its back, keep the lure stationary and mesmerize the dog with a relaxing tummy rub.

To teach *rollover-stay* when the dog is standing or moving, say "Fido, bang!" and give the appropriate hand signal (with index finger pointed and thumb cocked in true Sam Spade fashion), then in one fluid movement lure him to first lie down and then rollover-stay as above.

Teaching the dog to *stay* in each of the above four positions becomes a piece of cake after first teaching the dog not to worry at the toy or treat training lure. This is best accomplished by hand feeding dinner kibble. Hold a piece of kibble firmly in your hand and softly instruct "Off!" Ignore any licking and slobbering *for however long the dog worries at the treat*, but say "Take it!" and offer the kibble *the instant* the dog breaks contact with his muzzle. Repeat this a few times, and then up the ante and insist the dog remove his muzzle for one whole second before offering the kibble. Then progressively refine your criteria and have the dog not touch your hand (or treat) for longer and longer periods on each trial, such as for two seconds, four seconds, then six, ten, fifteen, twenty, thirty seconds and so on. The dog soon learns: (1) worrying at the treat never gets results, whereas (2) noncontact is often rewarded after a variable time lapse.

Teaching *"Off!"* has many useful applications in its own right. Additionally, instructing the dog not to touch a training lure often produces spontaneous and magical stays. Request the dog to stand-stay, for example, and not to touch the lure. At first set your sights on a short two-second stay before rewarding the dog. (Remember, every long journey begins with a single step.) However, on subsequent trials, gradually and progressively increase the length of stay required to receive a reward. In no time at all your dog will stand calmly for a minute or so.

Relevancy Training

Once you have taught the dog what you expect her to do when requested to come, sit, lie down, stand, rollover and stay, the time is right to teach the dog *why* she should comply with your wishes. The secret is to have many (*many*) extremely short training interludes (two to five seconds each) at numerous (*numerous*) times during the course of the dog's day. Especially work with the dog immediately *before* the dog's good times and *during* the dog's good times. For example, ask your dog to sit and/or lie down each time before opening doors, serving meals, offering treats and tummy rubs; ask the dog to perform a few controlled doggy push-ups before letting her off-leash or throwing a tennis ball; and perhaps request the dog to sit-down-sit-stand-down-stand-rollover before inviting her to cuddle on the couch.

Similarly, request the dog to sit many times during play or on walks, and in no time at all the dog will be only too pleased to follow your instructions because he has learned that a compliant response heralds all sorts of goodies. Basically all you are trying to teach the dog is how to say please: "Please throw the tennis ball. Please may I snuggle on the couch."

Remember, whereas it is important to keep training interludes short, it is equally important to have many short sessions each and every day. The shortest (and most useful) session comprises asking the dog to sit and then go play during a play session. When trained this way, your dog will soon associate training with good times. In fact, the dog may be unable to distinguish between training and good times and, indeed, there should be no distinction. The warped concept that training involves forcing the dog to comply and/or dominating his will is totally at odds with the picture of a truly well-trained dog. In reality, enjoying a game of training with a dog is no different from enjoying a game of backgammon or tennis with a friend; and walking with a dog should be no different from strolling with buddies on the golf course.

Walk by Your Side

Many people attempt to teach a dog to heel by putting him on a leash and physically correcting the dog when he makes mistakes. There are a number of things seriously wrong with this approach, the first being that most people do not want precision heeling; rather, they simply want the dog to follow or walk by their side. Second, when physically restrained during "training," even though the dog may grudgingly mope by your side when "handcuffed" on leash, let's see what happens when he is off leash. History! The dog is in the next county because he never enjoyed walking with you on leash and you have no control over him off leash. So let's just teach the dog off leash from the outset to *want* to walk with us. Third, if the dog has not been trained to heel, it is a trifle hasty to think about punishing the poor dog for making mistakes and breaking heeling rules he didn't even know existed. This is simply not fair! Surely, if the dog had been adequately taught how to heel, he would seldom make mistakes and hence there would be no need to correct the dog. Remember, each mistake and each correction (punishment) advertise the trainer's inadequacy, not the dog's. The dog is not stubborn, he is not stupid and he is not bad. Even if he were, he would still require training, so let's train him properly.

Let's teach the dog to *enjoy* following us and to *want* to walk by our side offleash. Then it will be easier to teach high-precision off-leash heeling patterns if desired. After attaching the leash for safety on outdoor walks, but before going anywhere, it is necessary to teach the dog specifically not to pull. Now it will be much easier to teach on-leash walking and heeling because the dog already wants to walk with you, he is familiar with the desired walking and heeling positions and he knows not to pull.

FOLLOWING

Start by training your dog to follow you. Many puppies will follow if you simply walk away from them and maybe click your fingers or chuckle. Adult dogs may require additional enticement to stimulate them to follow, such as a training lure or, at the very least, a lively trainer. To teach the dog to follow: (1) keep walking and (2) walk away from the dog. If the dog attempts to lead or lag, change pace; slow down if the dog forges too far ahead, but speed up if he lags too far behind. Say "Steady!" or "Easy!" each time before you slow down and "Quickly!" or "Hustle!" each time before you speed up, and the dog will learn to change pace on cue. If the dog lags or leads too far, or if he wanders right or left, simply walk quickly in the opposite direction and maybe even run away from the dog and hide.

Practicing is a lot of fun; you can set up a course in your home, yard or park to do this. Indoors, entice the dog to follow upstairs, into a bedroom, into the bathroom, downstairs, around the living room couch, zig-zagging between dining room chairs and into the kitchen for dinner. Outdoors, get the dog to follow around park benches, trees, shrubs and along walkways and lines in the grass. (For safety outdoors, it is advisable to attach a long line on the dog, but never exert corrective tension on the line.)

Remember, following has a lot to do with attitude—*your* attitude! Most probably your dog will *not* want to follow Mr. Grumpy Troll with the personality of wilted lettuce. Lighten up—walk with a jaunty step, whistle a happy tune, sing, skip and tell jokes to your dog and he will be right there by your side.

BY YOUR SIDE

It is smart to train the dog to walk close on one side or the other—either side will do, your choice. When walking, jogging or cycling, it is generally bad news to have the dog suddenly cut in front of you. In fact, I train my dogs to walk "By my side" and "Other side"—both very useful instructions. It is possible to position the dog fairly accurately by looking to the appropriate side and clicking your fingers or slapping your thigh on that side. A precise positioning may be attained by holding a training lure, such as a chewtoy, tennis ball, or food treat. Stop and stand still several times throughout the walk, just as you would when window shopping or meeting a friend. Use the lure to make sure the dog slows down and stays close whenever you stop.

When teaching the dog to heel, we generally want her to sit in heel position when we stop. Teach heel

Using a toy to teach sit-heel-sit sequences: 1) "Phoenix, heel!" Standing still, move lure up and back over dog's muzzle.... 2) To position dog sitting in heel position on your left side. 3) "Phoenix, heel!" wagging lure in left hand. Change lure to right hand in preparation for sit signal.

position at the standstill and the dog will learn that the default heel position is sitting by your side (left or right—your choice, unless you wish to compete in obedience trials, in which case the dog must heel on the left).

Several times a day, stand up and call your dog to come and sit in heel position—"Fido, heel!" For example, instruct the dog to come to heel each time there are commercials on TV, or each time you turn a page of a novel, and the dog will get it in a single evening.

Practice straight-line heeling and turns separately. With the dog sitting at heel, teach him to turn in place. After each quarter-turn, half-turn or full turn in place, lure the dog to sit at heel. Now it's time for short straight-line heeling sequences, no more than a few steps at a time. Always think of heeling in terms of Sit-Heel-Sit sequences—start and end with the dog in position and do your best to keep him there when moving. Progressively increase the number of steps in each sequence. When the dog remains close for 20 yards of straight-line heeling, it is time to add a few turns and then sign up for a happy-heeling obedience class to get some advice from the experts.

4) Use hand signal only to lure dog to sit as you stop. Eventually, dog will sit automatically at heel whenever you stop. 5) "Good dog!"

NO PULLING ON LEASH

You can start teaching your dog not to pull on leash anywhere—in front of the television or outdoors—but regardless of location, you must not take a single step with tension in the leash. For a reason known only to dogs, even just a couple of paces of pulling on leash is intrinsically motivating and diabolically rewarding. Instead, attach the leash to the dog's collar, grasp the other end firmly with both hands held close to your chest, and stand still—do not budge an inch. Have somebody watch you with a stopwatch to time your progress, or else you will never believe this will work and so you will not even try the exercise, and your shoulder and the dog's neck will be traumatized for years to come.

Stand still and wait for the dog to stop pulling, and to sit and/or lie down. All dogs stop pulling and sit eventually. Most take only a couple of minutes; the all-time record is 22 $\frac{1}{5}$ minutes. Time how long it takes. Gently praise the dog when he stops pulling, and as soon as he sits, enthusiastically praise the dog and take just one step forwards, then immediately stand still. This single step usually demonstrates the ballistic reinforcing nature of pulling on leash; most dogs explode to the end of the leash, so be prepared for the strain. Stand firm and wait for the dog to sit again. Repeat this half a dozen times and you will probably notice a progressive reduction in the force of the dog's one-step explosions and a radical reduction in the time it takes for the dog to sit each time.

As the dog learns "Sit we go" and "Pull we stop," she will begin to walk forward calmly with each single step and automatically sit when you stop. Now try two steps before you stop. Wooooooo! Scary! When the dog has mastered two steps at a time, try for three. After each success, progressively increase the number of steps in the sequence: try four steps and then six, eight, ten and twenty steps before stopping. Congratulations! You are now walking the dog on leash.

Whenever walking with the dog (off leash or on leash), make sure you stop periodically to practice a few position commands and stays before instructing the dog to "Walk on!" (Remember, you want the dog to be compliant everywhere, not just in the kitchen when his dinner is at hand.) For example, stopping every 25 yards to briefly train the dog amounts to over 200 training interludes within a single three-mile stroll. And each training session is in a different location. You will not believe the improvement within just the first mile of the first walk.

To put it another way, integrating training into a walk offers 200 separate opportunities to use the continuance of the walk as a reward to reinforce the dog's education. Moreover, some training interludes may comprise continuing education for the dog's walking skills: Alternate short periods of the dog walking calmly by your side with periods when the dog is allowed to sniff and investigate the environment. Now sniffing odors on the grass and meeting other dogs become rewards which reinforce the dog's calm and mannerly demeanor. Good Lord! Whatever next? Many enjoyable walks together of course. Happy trails!

THE IMPORTANCE OF TRICKS

Nothing will improve a dog's quality of life better than having a few tricks under its belt. Teaching any trick expands the dog's vocabulary, which facilitates communication and improves the owner's control. Also, specific tricks help prevent and resolve specific behavior problems. For example, by teaching the dog to fetch his toys, the dog learns carrying a toy makes the owner happy and, therefore, will be more likely to chew his toy than other inappropriate items.

More important, teaching tricks prompts owners to lighten up and train with a sunny disposition. Really, tricks should be no different from any other behaviors we put on cue. But they are. When teaching tricks, owners have a much sweeter attitude, which in turn motivates the dog and improves her willingness to comply. The dog feels tricks are a blast, but formal commands are a drag. In fact, tricks are so enjoyable, they may be used as rewards in training by asking the dog to come, sit and down-stay and then rollover for a tummy rub. Go on, try it: Crack a smile and even giggle when the dog promptly and willingly lies down and stays.

Most important, performing tricks prompts onlookers to smile and giggle. Many people are scared of dogs, especially large ones. And nothing can be more off-putting for a dog than to be constantly confronted by strangers who don't like him because of his size or the way he looks. Uneasy people put the dog on edge, causing him to back off and bark, only frightening people all the more. And so a vicious circle develops, with the people's fear fueling the dog's fear *and vice versa*. Instead, tie a pink ribbon to your dog's collar and practice all sorts of tricks on walks and in the park, and you will be pleasantly amazed how it changes people's attitudes toward your friendly dog. The dog's repertoire of tricks is limited only by the trainer's imagination. Below I have described three of my favorites:

SPEAK AND SHUSH

The training sequence involved in teaching a dog to bark on request is no different from that used when training any behavior on cue: request—lure—response—reward. As always, the secret of success lies in finding an effective lure. If the dog always barks at the doorbell, for example, say "Rover, speak!", have an accomplice ring the doorbell, then reward the dog for barking. After a few woofs, ask Rover to "Shush!", waggle a food treat under his nose (to entice him to sniff and thus to shush), praise him when quiet and eventually offer the treat as a reward. Alternate "Speak" and "Shush," progressively increasing the length of shush-time between each barking bout.

PLAYBOW

With the dog standing, say "Bow!" and lower the food lure (palm upwards) to rest between the dog's forepaws. Praise as the dog lowers her forequarters and sternum to the ground (as when teaching the down), but then lure the dog to stand and offer the treat. On successive trials, gradually increase the length of time the dog is required to remain in the playbow posture in order to gain a food reward. If the dog's rear end collapses into a down, say nothing and offer no reward; simply start over.

BE A BEAR

With the dog sitting backed into a corner to prevent him from toppling over backwards, say "Be a Bear!" With bent paw and palm down, raise a lure upwards and backwards along the top of the dog's muzzle. Praise the dog when he sits up on his haunches and offer the treat as a reward. To prevent the dog from standing on his hind legs, keep the lure closer to the dog's muzzle. On each trial, progressively increase the length of time the dog is required to sit up to receive a food reward. Since lure/ reward training is so easy, teach the dog to stand and walk on his hind legs as well!

Teaching "Be a Bear"

Getting
Active
with your Dog

by Bardi McLennan

Once you and your dog have graduated from basic obedience training and are beginning to work together as a team, you can take part in the growing world of dog activities. There are so many fun things to do with your dog! Just remember, people and dogs don't always learn at the same pace, so don't be upset if you (or your dog) need more than two basic training courses before your team becomes operational. Even smart dogs don't go straight to college from kindergarten!

Just as there are events geared to certain types of dogs, so there are ones that are more appealing to certain types of people. In some activities, you give the commands and your dog does the work (upland game hunting is one example), while in others, such as agility, you'll both get a workout. You may want to aim for prestigious titles to add to your dog's name, or you may want nothing more than the sheer enjoyment of being around other people and their dogs. Passive or active, participation has its own rewards.

Consider your dog's physical capabilities when looking into any of the canine activities. It's easy to see that a Basset Hound is not built for the racetrack, nor would a Chihuahua be the breed of choice for pulling a sled. A loyal dog will attempt almost anything you ask him to do, so it is up to you to know your

All dogs seem to love playing flyball.

dog's limitations. A dog must be physically sound in order to compete at any level in athletic activities, and being mentally sound is a definite plus. Advanced age, however, may not be a deterrent. Many dogs still hunt and herd at ten or twelve years of age. It's entirely possible for dogs to be "fit at 50." Take your dog for a checkup, explain to your vet the type of activity you have in mind and be guided by his or her findings.

You needn't be restricted to breed-specific sports if it's only fun you're after. Certain AKC activities are limited to designated breeds; however, as each new trial, test or sport has grown in popularity, so has the variety of breeds encouraged to participate at a fun level.

But don't shortchange your fun, or that of your dog, by thinking only of the basic function of her breed. Once a dog has learned how to learn, she can be taught to do just about anything as long as the size of the dog is right for the job and you both think it is fun and rewarding. In other words, you are a team.

To get involved in any of the activities detailed in this chapter, look for the names and addresses of the organizations that sponsor them in Chapter 13. You can also ask your breeder or a local dog trainer for contacts.

You can compete in obedience trials with a well trained dog.

Official American Kennel Club Activities

The following tests and trials are some of the events sanctioned by the AKC and sponsored by various dog clubs. Your dog's expertise will be rewarded with impressive titles. You can participate just for fun, or be competitive and go for those awards.

OBEDIENCE

Training classes begin with pups as young as three months of age in kindergarten puppy training, then advance to pre-novice (all exercises on lead) and go on to novice, which is where you'll start off-lead work. In obedience classes dogs learn to sit, stay, heel and come through a variety of exercises. Once you've got the basics down, you can enter obedience trials and work toward earning your dog's first degree, a C.D. (Companion Dog).

The next level is called "Open," in which jumps and retrieves perk up the dog's interest. Passing grades in competition at this level earn a C.D.X. (Companion Dog Excellent). Beyond that lies the goal of the most ambitious—Utility (U.D. and even U.D.X. or OTCh, an Obedience Champion).

AGILITY

All dogs can participate in the latest canine sport to have gained worldwide popularity for its fun and excitement, agility. It began in England as a canine version of horse show-jumping, but because dogs are more agile and able to perform on verbal commands, extra feats were added such as climbing, balancing and racing through tunnels or in and out of weave poles.

Many of the obstacles (regulation or homemade) can be set up in your own backyard. If the agility bug bites, you could end up in international competition!

For starters, your dog should be obedience trained, even though, in the beginning, the lessons may all be taught on lead. Once the dog understands the commands (and you do, too), it's as easy as guiding the dog over a prescribed course, one obstacle at a time. In competition, the race is against the clock, so wear your running shoes! The dog starts with 200 points and the judge deducts for infractions and misadventures along the way.

All dogs seem to love agility and respond to it as if they were being turned loose in a playground paradise. Your dog's enthusiasm will be contagious; agility turns into great fun for dog and owner.

FIELD TRIALS AND HUNTING TESTS

There are field trials and hunting tests for the sporting breeds—retrievers, spaniels and pointing breeds, and for some hounds—Bassets, Beagles and Dachshunds. Field trials are competitive events that test a dog's ability to perform the functions for which she was bred. Hunting tests, which are open to retrievers,

---

TITLES AWARDED BY THE AKC

Conformation: Ch. (Champion)

Obedience: CD (Companion Dog); CDX (Companion Dog Excellent); UD (Utility Dog); UDX (Utility Dog Excellent); OTCh. (Obedience Trial Champion)

Field: JH (Junior Hunter); SH (Senior Hunter); MH (Master Hunter); AFCh. (Amateur Field Champion); FCh. (Field Champion)

Lure Coursing: JC (Junior Courser); SC (Senior Courser)

Herding: HT (Herding Tested); PT (Pre-Trial Tested); HS (Herding Started); HI (Herding Intermediate); HX (Herding Excellent); HCh. (Herding Champion)

Tracking: TD (Tracking Dog); TDX (Tracking Dog Excellent)

Agility: NAD (Novice Agility); OAD (Open Agility); ADX (Agility Excellent); MAX (Master Agility)

Earthdog Tests: JE (Junior Earthdog); SE (Senior Earthdog); ME (Master Earthdog)

Canine Good Citizen: CGC

Combination: DC (Dual Champion—Ch. and Fch.); TC (Triple Champion—Ch., Fch., and OTCh.)

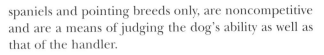
spaniels and pointing breeds only, are noncompetitive and are a means of judging the dog's ability as well as that of the handler.

Hunting is a very large and complex part of canine sports, and if you own one of the breeds that hunts, the events are a great treat for your dog and you. He gets to do what he was bred for, and you get to work with him and watch him do it. You'll be proud of and amazed at what your dog can do.

Fortunately, the AKC publishes a series of booklets on these events, which outline the rules and regulations and include a glossary of the sometimes complicated terms. The AKC also publishes newsletters for field trialers and hunting test enthusiasts. The United Kennel Club (UKC) also has informative materials for the hunter and his dog.

Retrievers and other sporting breeds get to do what they're bred to in hunting tests.

HERDING TESTS AND TRIALS

Herding, like hunting, dates back to the first known uses man made of dogs. The interest in herding today is widespread, and if you own a herding breed, you can join in the activity. Herding dogs are tested for their natural skills to keep a flock of ducks, sheep or cattle together. If your dog shows potential, you can start at the testing level, where your dog can earn a title for showing an inherent herding ability. With training you can advance to the trial level, where your dog should be capable of controlling even difficult livestock in diverse situations.

LURE COURSING

The AKC Tests and Trials for Lure Coursing are open to traditional sighthounds—Greyhounds, Whippets,

Borzoi, Salukis, Afghan Hounds, Ibizan Hounds and Scottish Deerhounds—as well as to Basenjis and Rhodesian Ridgebacks. Hounds are judged on overall ability, follow, speed, agility and endurance. This is possibly the most exciting of the trials for spectators, because the speed and agility of the dogs is awesome to watch as they chase the lure (or "course") in heats of two or three dogs at a time.

TRACKING

Tracking is another activity in which almost any dog can compete because every dog that sniffs the ground when taken outdoors is, in fact, tracking. The hard part comes when the rules as to what, when and where the dog tracks are determined by a person, not the dog! Tracking tests cover a large area of fields, woods and roads. The tracks are

laid hours before the dogs go to work on them, and include "tricks" like cross-tracks and sharp turns. If you're interested in search-and-rescue work, this is the place to start.

This tracking dog is hot on the trail.

EARTHDOG TESTS FOR SMALL TERRIERS AND DACHSHUNDS

These tests are open to Australian, Bedlington, Border, Cairn, Dandie Dinmont, Smooth and Wire Fox, Lakeland, Norfolk, Norwich, Scottish, Sealyham, Skye, Welsh and West Highland White Terriers as well as Dachshunds. The dogs need no prior training for this terrier sport. There is a qualifying test on the day of the event, so dog and handler learn the rules on the spot. These tests, or "digs," sometimes end with informal races in the late afternoon.

133

Here are some of the extracurricular obedience and racing activities that are not regulated by the AKC or UKC, but are generally run by clubs or a group of dog fanciers and are often open to all.

Canine Freestyle This activity is something new on the scene and is variously likened to dancing, dressage or ice skating. It is meant to show the athleticism of the dog, but also requires showmanship on the part of the dog's handler. If you and your dog like to ham it up for friends, you might want to look into freestyle.

Lure coursing lets sighthounds do what they do best—run!

Scent Hurdle Racing Scent hurdle racing is purely a fun activity sponsored by obedience clubs with members forming competing teams. The height of the hurdles is based on the size of the shortest dog on the team. On a signal, one team dog is released on each of two side-by-side courses and must clear every hurdle before picking up its own dumbbell from a platform and returning over the jumps to the handler. As each dog returns, the next on that team is sent. Of course, that is what the dogs are supposed to do. When the dogs improvise (going under or around the hurdles, stealing another dog's dumbbell, and so forth), it no doubt frustrates the handlers, but just adds to the fun for everyone else.

Flyball This type of racing is similar, but after negotiating the four hurdles, the dog comes to a flyball box, steps on a lever that releases a tennis ball into the air, catches the ball and returns over the hurdles to the starting point. This game also becomes extremely fun for spectators because the dogs sometimes cheat by catching a ball released by the dog in the next lane. Three titles can be earned—Flyball Dog (F.D.), Flyball Dog Excellent (F.D.X.) and Flyball Dog Champion (Fb.D.Ch.)—all awarded by the North American Flyball Association, Inc.

Dogsledding The name conjures up the Rocky Mountains or the frigid North, but you can find dogsled clubs in such unlikely spots as Maryland, North Carolina and Virginia! Dogsledding is primarily for the Nordic breeds such as the Alaskan Malamutes, Siberian Huskies and Samoyeds, but other breeds can try. There are some practical backyard applications to this sport, too. With parental supervision, almost any strong dog could pull a child's sled.

Coming over the A-frame on an agility course.

These are just some of the many recreational ways you can get to know and understand your multifaceted dog better and have fun doing it.

chapter 10

Your Dog
and your
Family

by Bardi McLennan

Adding a dog automatically increases your family by one, no matter whether you live alone in an apartment or are part of a mother, father and six kids household. The single-person family is fair game for numerous and varied canine misconceptions as to who is dog and who pays the bills, whereas a dog in a houseful of children will consider himself to be just one of the gang, littermates all. One dog and one child may give a dog reason to believe they are both kids or both dogs.

Either interpretation requires parental supervision and sometimes speedy intervention.

As soon as one paw goes through the door into your home, Rufus (or Rufina) has to make many adjustments to become a part of your family. Your job is to make him fit in as painlessly as possible. An older dog may have some frame of reference from past experience, but to a 10-week-old puppy, everything is brand new: people, furniture, stairs, when and where people eat, sleep or watch TV, his own place and everyone else's space, smells, sounds, outdoors—everything!

Puppies, and newly acquired dogs of any age, do not need what we think of as "freedom." If you leave a new dog or puppy loose in the house, you will almost certainly return to chaotic destruction and the dog will forever after equate your homecoming with a time of punishment to be dreaded. It is unfair to give your dog what amounts to "freedom to get into trouble." Instead, confine him to a crate for brief periods of your absence (up to three or four hours) and, for the long haul, a workday for example, confine him to one untrashable area with his own toys, a bowl of water and a radio left on (low) in another room.

Lots of pets get along with each other just fine.

For the first few days, when not confined, put Rufus on a long leash tied to your wrist or waist. This umbilical cord method enables the dog to learn all about you from your body language and voice, and to learn by his own actions which things in the house are NO! and which ones are rewarded by "Good dog." House-training will be easier with the pup always by your side. Speaking of which, accidents do happen. That goal of "completely housetrained" takes up to a year, or the length of time it takes the pup to mature.

The All-Adult Family

Most dogs in an adults-only household today are likely to be latchkey pets, with no one home all day but the dog. When you return after a tough day on the job, the dog can and should be your relaxation therapy. But going home can instead be a daily frustration.

Separation anxiety is a very common problem for the dog in a working household. It may begin with whines and barks of loneliness, but it will soon escalate into a frenzied destruction derby. That is why it is so important to set aside the time to teach a dog to relax when left alone in his confined area and to understand that he can trust you to return.

Let the dog get used to your work schedule in easy stages. Confine him to one room and go in and out of that room over and over again. Be casual about it. No physical, voice or eye contact. When the pup no longer even notices your comings and goings, leave the house for varying lengths of time, returning to stay home for a few minutes and gradually increasing the time away. This training can take days, but the dog is learning that you haven't left him forever and that he can trust you.

Any time you leave the dog, but especially during this training period, be casual about your departure. No anxiety-building fond farewells. Just "Bye" and go! Remember the "Good dog" when you return to find everything more or less as you left it.

If things are a mess (or even a disaster) when you return, greet the dog, take him outside to eliminate, and then put him in his crate while you clean up. Rant and rave in the shower! *Do not* punish the dog. You were not there when it happened, and the rule is: Only punish as you catch the dog in the act of wrongdoing. Obviously, it makes sense to get your latchkey puppy when you'll have a week or two to spend on these training essentials.

Family weekend activities should include Rufus whenever possible. Depending on the pup's age, now is the time for a long walk in the park, playtime in the backyard, a hike in the woods. Socializing is as important as health care, good food and physical exercise, so visiting Aunt Emma or Uncle Harry and the next-door neighbor's dog or cat is essential to developing an outgoing, friendly temperament in your pet.

If you are a single adult, socializing Rufus at home and away will prevent him from becoming overly protective of you (or just overly attached) and will also prevent such behavioral problems as dominance or fear of strangers.

Babies

Whether already here or on the way, babies figure larger than life in the eyes of a dog. If the dog is there first, let him in on all your baby preparations in the house. When baby arrives, let Rufus sniff any item of clothing that has been on the baby before Junior comes home. Then let Mom greet the dog first before introducing the new family member. Hold the baby down for the dog to see and sniff, but make sure someone's holding the dog on lead in case of any sudden moves. Don't play keep-away or tease the dog with the baby, which only invites undesirable jumping up.

The dog and the baby are "family," and for starters can be treated almost as equals. Things rapidly change, however, especially when baby takes to creeping around on all fours on the dog's turf or, better yet, has yummy pudding all over her face and hands! That's when a lot of things in the dog's and baby's lives become more separate than equal.

Dogs are perfect confidants.

Toddlers make terrible dog owners, but if you can't avoid the combination, use patient discipline (that is, positive teaching rather than punishment), and use time-outs before you run out of patience.

A dog and a baby (or toddler, or an assertive young child) should never be left alone together. Take the dog with you or confine him. With a baby or youngsters in the house, you'll have plenty of use for that wonderful canine safety device called a crate!

Young Children

Any dog in a house with kids will behave pretty much as the kids do, good or bad. But even good dogs and good children can get into trouble when play becomes rowdy and active.

Legs bobbing up and down, shrill voices screeching, a ball hurtling overhead, all add up to exuberant frustration for a dog who's just trying to be part of the gang. In a pack of puppies, any legs or toys being chased would be caught by a set of teeth, and all the pups involved would understand that is how the game is played. Kids do not understand this, nor do parents tolerate it. Bring Rufus indoors before you have reason to regret it. This is time-out, not a punishment.

Teach children how to play nicely with a puppy.

You can explain the situation to the children and tell them they must play quieter games until the puppy learns not to grab them with his mouth. Unfortunately, you can't explain it that easily to the dog. With adult supervision, they will learn how to play together.

Young children love to tease. Sticking their faces or wiggling their hands or fingers in the dog's face is teasing. To another person it might be just annoying, but it is threatening to a dog. There's another difference: We can make the child stop by an explanation, but the only way a dog can stop it is with a warning growl and then with teeth. Teasing is the major cause of children being bitten by their pets. Treat it seriously.

140

Older Children

The best age for a child to get a first dog is between the ages of 8 and 12. That's when kids are able to accept some real responsibility for their pet. Even so, take the child's vow of "I will never *ever* forget to feed (brush, walk, etc.) the dog" for what it's worth: a child's good intention at that moment. Most kids today have extra lessons, soccer practice, Little League, ballet, and so forth piled on top of school schedules. There will be many times when Mom will have to come to the dog's rescue. "I walked the dog for you so you can set the table for me" is one way to get around a missed appointment without laying on blame or guilt.

Kids in this age group make excellent obedience trainers because they are into the teaching/learning process themselves and they lack the self-consciousness of adults. Attending a dog show is something the whole family can enjoy, and watching Junior Showmanship may catch the eye of the kids. Older children can begin to get involved in many of the recreational activities that were reviewed in the previous chapter. Some of the agility obstacles, for example, can be set up in the backyard as a family project (with an adult making sure all the equipment is safe and secure for the dog).

Older kids are also beginning to look to the future, and may envision themselves as veterinarians or trainers or show dog handlers or writers of the next Lassie best-seller. Dogs are perfect confidants for these dreams. They won't tell a soul.

Other Pets

Introduce all pets tactfully. In a dog/cat situation, hold the dog, not the cat. Let two dogs meet on neutral turf—a stroll in the park or a walk down the street—with both on loose leads to permit all the normal canine ways of saying hello, including routine sniffing, circling, more sniffing, and so on. Small creatures such as hamsters, chinchillas or mice must be kept safe from their natural predators (dogs and cats).

Festive Family Occasions

Parties are great for people, but not necessarily for puppies. Until all the guests have arrived, put the dog in his crate or in a room where he won't be disturbed. A socialized dog can join the fun later as long as he's not underfoot, annoying guests or into the hors d'oeuvres.

There are a few dangers to consider, too. Doors opening and closing can allow a puppy to slip out unnoticed in the confusion, and you'll be organizing a search party instead of playing host or hostess. Party food and buffet service are not for dogs. Let Rufus party in his crate with a nice big dog biscuit.

At Christmas time, not only are tree decorations dangerous and breakable (and perhaps family heirlooms), but extreme caution should be taken with the lights, cords and outlets for the tree lights and any other festive lighting. Occasionally a dog lifts a leg, ignoring the fact that the tree is indoors. To avoid this, use a canine repellent, made for gardens, on the tree. Or keep him out of the tree room unless supervised. And whatever you do, *don't* invite trouble by hanging his toys on the tree!

Car Travel

Before you plan a vacation by car or RV with Rufus, be sure he enjoys car travel. Nothing spoils a holiday quicker than a carsick dog! Work within the dog's comfort level. Get in the car with the dog in his crate or attached to a canine car safety belt and just sit there until he relaxes. That's all. Next time, get in the car, turn on the engine and go nowhere. Just sit. When that is okay, turn on the engine and go around the block. Now you can go for a ride and include a stop where you get out, leaving the dog for a minute or two.

On a warm day, always park in the shade and leave windows open several inches. And return quickly. It only takes 10 minutes for a car to become an overheated steel death trap.

Motel or Pet Motel?

Not all motels or hotels accept pets, but you have a much better choice today than even a few years ago. To find a dog-friendly lodging, look at *On the Road Again With Man's Best Friend*, a series of directories that detail bed and breakfasts, inns, family resorts and other hotels/motels. Some places require a refundable deposit to cover any damage incurred by the dog. More B&Bs accept pets now, but some restrict the size.

If taking Rufus with you is not feasible, check out boarding kennels in your area. Your veterinarian may offer this service, or recommend a kennel or two he or she is familiar with. Go see the facilities for yourself, ask about exercise, diet, housing, and so on. Or, if you'd rather have Rufus stay home, look into bonded petsitters, many of whom will also bring in the mail and water your plants.

Your Dog
and your
Community

by Bardi McLennan

Step outside your home with your dog and you are no longer just family, you are both part of your community. This is when the phrase "responsible pet ownership" takes on serious implications. For starters, it means you pick up after your dog—not just occasionally, but every time your dog eliminates away from home. That means you have joined the Plastic Baggy Brigade! You always have plastic sandwich bags in your pocket and several in the car. It means you teach your kids how to use them, too. If you think this is "yucky," just imagine what

the person (a non-doggy person) who inadvertently steps in the mess thinks!

144

Your responsibility extends to your neighbors: To their ears (no annoying barking); to their property (their garbage, their lawn, their flower beds, their cat—especially their cat); to their kids (on bikes, at play); to their kids' toys and sports equipment.

There are numerous dog-related laws, ranging from simple dog licensing and leash laws to those holding you liable for any physical injury or property damage done by your dog. These laws are in place to protect everyone in the community, including you and your dog. There are town ordinances and state laws which are by no means the same in all towns or all states. Ignorance of the law won't get you off the hook. The time to find out what the laws are where you live is now.

Be sure your dog's license is current. This is not just a good local ordinance, it can make the difference between finding your lost dog or not. Many states now require proof of rabies vaccination and that the dog has been spayed or neutered before issuing a license. At the same time, keep up the dog's annual immunizations.

Dressing your dog up makes him appealing to strangers.

Never let your dog run loose in the neighborhood. This will not only keep you on the right side of the leash law, it's the outdoor version of the rule about not giving your dog "freedom to get into trouble."

Good Canine Citizen

Sometimes it's hard for a dog's owner to assess whether or not the dog is sufficiently socialized to be accepted by the community at large. Does Rufus or Rufina display good, controlled behavior in public? The AKC's Canine Good Citizen program is available through many dog organizations. If your dog passes the test, the title "CGC" is earned.

The overall purpose is to turn your dog into a good neighbor and to teach you about your responsibility to your community as a dog owner. Here are the ten things your dog must do willingly:

1. Allow a stranger to handle him or her as a groomer or veterinarian would.
2. Accept a stranger stopping to chat with you.
3. Walk nicely on a loose lead.
4. Walk calmly through a crowd.
5. Sit and be petted by a stranger.
6. Sit and down on command.
7. Stay put when you move away.
8. Casually greet another dog.
9. React confidently to distractions.
10. Accept being tied up in a strange place and left alone for a few minutes.

Schools and Dogs

Schools are getting involved with pet ownership on an educational level. It has been proven that children who are kind to animals are humane in their attitude toward other people as adults.

A dog is a child's best friend, and so children are often primary pet owners, if not the primary caregivers. Unfortunately, they are also the ones most often bitten by dogs. This occurs due to a lack of understanding that pets, no matter how sweet, cuddly and loving, are still animals. Schools, along with parents, dog clubs, dog fanciers and the AKC, are working to change all that with video programs for children not only in grade school, but in the nursery school and pre-kindergarten age group. Teaching youngsters how to be responsible dog owners is important community work. When your dog has a CGC, volunteer to take part in an educational classroom event put on by your dog club.

Boy Scout Merit Badge

A Merit Badge for Dog Care can be earned by any Boy Scout ages 11 to 18. The requirements are not easy, but amount to a complete course in responsible dog care and general ownership. Here are just a few of the things a Scout must do to earn that badge:

> Point out ten parts of the dog using the correct names.

> Give a report (signed by parent or guardian) on your care of the dog (feeding, food used, housing, exercising, grooming and bathing), plus what has been done to keep the dog healthy.

> Explain the right way to obedience train a dog, and demonstrate three comments.

> Several of the requirements have to do with health care, including first aid, handling a hurt dog, and the dangers of home treatment for a serious ailment.

> The final requirement is to know the local laws and ordinances involving dogs.

There are similar programs for Girl Scouts and 4-H members.

Local Clubs

Local dog clubs are no longer in existence just to put on a yearly dog show. Today, they are apt to be the hub of the community's involvement with pets. Dog clubs conduct educational forums with big-name speakers, stage demonstrations of canine talent in a busy mall and take dogs of various breeds to schools for class-room discussion.

The quickest way to feel accepted as a member in a club is to volunteer your services! Offer to help with something—anything—and watch your popularity (and your interest) grow.

Therapy Dogs

Once your dog has earned that essential CGC and reliably demonstrates a steady, calm temperament, you could look into what therapy dogs are doing in your area.

Therapy dogs go with their owners to visit patients at hospitals or nursing homes, generally remaining on leash but able to coax a pat from a stiffened hand, a smile from a blank face, a few words from sealed lips or a hug from someone in need of love.

Nursing homes cover a wide range of patient care. Some specialize in care of the elderly, some in the treatment of specific illnesses, some in physical therapy. Children's facilities also welcome visits from trained therapy dogs for boosting morale in their pediatric patients. Hospice care for the terminally ill and the at-home care of AIDS patients are other areas

Your dog can make a difference in lots of lives.

where this canine visiting is desperately needed. Therapy dog training comes first.

There is a lot more involved than just taking your nice friendly pooch to someone's bedside. Doing therapy dog work involves your own emotional stability as well as that of your dog. But once you have met all the requirements for this work, making the rounds once a week or once a month with your therapy dog is possibly the most rewarding of all community activities.

Disaster Aid

This community service is definitely not for everyone, partly because it is time-consuming. The initial training is rigorous, and there can be no let-up in the continuing workouts, because members are on call 24 hours a day to go wherever they are needed at a moment's notice. But if you think you would like to be able to assist in a disaster, look into search-and-rescue work. The network of search-and-rescue volunteers is worldwide, and all members of the American Rescue Dog Association (ARDA) who are qualified to do this work are volunteers who train and maintain their own dogs.

Physical Aid

Most people are familiar with Seeing Eye dogs, which serve as blind people's eyes, but not with all the other work that dogs are trained to do to assist the disabled. Dogs are also specially trained to pull wheelchairs, carry school books, pick up dropped objects, open and close doors. Some also are ears for the deaf. All these assistance-trained dogs, by the way, are allowed anywhere "No Pet" signs exist (as are therapy dogs when properly identified). Getting started in any of this fascinating work requires a background in dog training and canine behavior, but there are also volunteer jobs ranging from answering the phone to cleaning out kennels to providing a foster home for a puppy. You have only to ask.

Making the rounds with your therapy dog can be very rewarding.

part four

Beyond
the
Basics

chapter 12

Recommended Reading

Books

ABOUT HEALTH CARE

Ackerman, Lowell. *Guide to Skin and Haircoat Problems in Dogs.* Loveland, Colo.: Alpine Publications, 1994.

Alderton, David. *The Dog Care Manual.* Hauppauge, N.Y.: Barron's Educational Series, Inc., 1986.

American Kennel Club. *American Kennel Club Dog Care and Training.* New York: Howell Book House, 1991.

Bamberger, Michelle, DVM. *Help! The Quick Guide to First Aid for Your Dog.* New York: Howell Book House, 1995.

Carlson, Delbert, DVM, and James Giffin, MD. *Dog Owner's Home Veterinary Handbook.* New York: Howell Book House, 1992.

DeBitetto, James, DVM, and Sarah Hodgson. *You & Your Puppy.* New York: Howell Book House, 1995.

Humphries, Jim, DVM. *Dr. Jim's Animal Clinic for Dogs.* New York: Howell Book House, 1994.

McGinnis, Terri. *The Well Dog Book.* New York: Random House, 1991.

Pitcairn, Richard and Susan. *Natural Health for Dogs.* Emmaus, Pa.: Rodale Press, 1982.

ABOUT DOG SHOWS

Hall, Lynn. *Dog Showing for Beginners.* New York: Howell Book House, 1994.

Nichols, Virginia Tuck. *How to Show Your Own Dog.* Neptune, N. J.: TFH, 1970.

Vanacore, Connie. *Dog Showing, An Owner's Guide.* New York: Howell Book House, 1990.

ABOUT TRAINING

Ammen, Amy. *Training in No Time*. New York: Howell Book House, 1995.

Baer, Ted. *Communicating With Your Dog*. Hauppauge, N.Y.: Barron's Educational Series, Inc., 1989.

Benjamin, Carol Lea. *Dog Problems*. New York: Howell Book House, 1989.

Benjamin, Carol Lea. *Dog Training for Kids*. New York: Howell Book House, 1988.

Benjamin, Carol Lea. *Mother Knows Best*. New York: Howell Book House, 1985.

Benjamin, Carol Lea. *Surviving Your Dog's Adolescence*. New York: Howell Book House, 1993.

Bohnenkamp, Gwen. *Manners for the Modern Dog*. San Francisco: Perfect Paws, 1990.

Dibra, Bashkim. *Dog Training by Bash*. New York: Dell, 1992.

Dunbar, Ian, PhD, MRCVS. *Dr. Dunbar's Good Little Dog Book*, James & Kenneth Publishers, 2140 Shattuck Ave. #2406, Berkeley, Calif. 94704. (510) 658–8588. Order from the publisher.

Dunbar, Ian, PhD, MRCVS. *How to Teach a New Dog Old Tricks*, James & Kenneth Publishers. Order from the publisher; address above.

Dunbar, Ian, PhD, MRCVS, and Gwen Bohnenkamp. Booklets on *Preventing Aggression; Housetraining; Chewing; Digging; Barking; Socialization; Fearfulness; and Fighting*, James & Kenneth Publishers. Order from the publisher; address above.

Evans, Job Michael. *People, Pooches and Problems*. New York: Howell Book House, 1991.

Kilcommons, Brian and Sarah Wilson. *Good Owners, Great Dogs*. New York: Warner Books, 1992.

McMains, Joel M. *Dog Logic—Companion Obedience*. New York: Howell Book House, 1992.

Rutherford, Clarice and David H. Neil, MRCVS. *How to Raise a Puppy You Can Live With*. Loveland, Colo.: Alpine Publications, 1982.

Volhard, Jack and Melissa Bartlett. *What All Good Dogs Should Know: The Sensible Way to Train*. New York: Howell Book House, 1991.

ABOUT BREEDING

Harris, Beth J. Finder. *Breeding a Litter, The Complete Book of Prenatal and Postnatal Care*. New York: Howell Book House, 1983.

Holst, Phyllis, DVM. *Canine Reproduction*. Loveland, Colo.: Alpine Publications, 1985.

Walkowicz, Chris and Bonnie Wilcox, DVM. *Successful Dog Breeding, The Complete Handbook of Canine Midwifery*. New York: Howell Book House, 1994.

About Activities

American Rescue Dog Association. *Search and Rescue Dogs*. New York: Howell Book House, 1991.

Barwig, Susan and Stewart Hilliard. *Schutzhund*. New York: Howell Book House, 1991.

Beaman, Arthur S. *Lure Coursing*. New York: Howell Book House, 1994.

Daniels, Julie. *Enjoying Dog Agility—From Backyard to Competition*. New York: Doral Publishing, 1990.

Davis, Kathy Diamond. *Therapy Dogs*. New York: Howell Book House, 1992.

Gallup, Davis Anne. *Running With Man's Best Friend*. Loveland, Colo.: Alpine Publications, 1986.

Habgood, Dawn and Robert. *On the Road Again With Man's Best Friend*. New England, Mid-Atlantic, West Coast and Southeast editions. Selective guides to area bed and breakfasts, inns, hotels and resorts that welcome guests and their dogs. New York: Howell Book House, 1995.

Holland, Vergil S. *Herding Dogs*. New York: Howell Book House, 1994.

LaBelle, Charlene G. *Backpacking With Your Dog*. Loveland, Colo.: Alpine Publications, 1993.

Simmons-Moake, Jane. *Agility Training, The Fun Sport for All Dogs*. New York: Howell Book House, 1991.

Spencer, James B. *Hup! Training Flushing Spaniels the American Way*. New York: Howell Book House, 1992.

Spencer, James B. *Point! Training the All-Seasons Birddog*. New York: Howell Book House, 1995.

Tarrant, Bill. *Training the Hunting Retriever*. New York: Howell Book House, 1991.

Volhard, Jack and Wendy. *The Canine Good Citizen*. New York: Howell Book House, 1994.

General Titles

Haggerty, Captain Arthur J. *How to Get Your Pet Into Show Business*. New York: Howell Book House, 1994.

McLennan, Bardi. *Dogs and Kids, Parenting Tips*. New York: Howell Book House, 1993.

Moran, Patti J. *Pet Sitting for Profit, A Complete Manual for Professional Success*. New York: Howell Book House, 1992.

Scalisi, Danny and Libby Moses. *When Rover Just Won't Do, Over 2,000
Suggestions for Naming Your Dog.* New York: Howell Book House, 1993.

Sife, Wallace, PhD. *The Loss of a Pet.* New York: Howell Book House,
1993.

Wrede, Barbara J. *Civilizing Your Puppy.* Hauppauge, N.Y.: Barron's
Educational Series, 1992.

Magazines

The AKC GAZETTE, The Official Journal for the Sport of Purebred Dogs.
American Kennel Club, 51 Madison Ave., New York, NY.

Bloodlines Journal. United Kennel Club, 100 E. Kilgore Rd.,
Kalamazoo, MI.

Dog Fancy. Fancy Publications, 3 Burroughs, Irvine, CA 92718

Dog World. Maclean Hunter Publishing Corp., 29 N. Wacker Dr.,
Chicago, IL 60606.

Videos

"SIRIUS Puppy Training," by Ian Dunbar, PhD, MRCVS. James &
Kenneth Publishers, 2140 Shattuck Ave. #2406, Berkeley, CA 94704.
Order from the publisher.

"Training the Companion Dog," from Dr. Dunbar's British TV
Series, James & Kenneth Publishers. (See address above).

The American Kennel Club produces videos on every breed of dog,
as well as on hunting tests, field trials and other areas of interest to
purebred dog owners. For more information, write to AKC/Video
Fulfillment, 5580 Centerview Dr., Suite 200, Raleigh, NC 27606.

chapter 13

Resources

Breed Clubs

Every breed recognized by the American Kennel Club has a national (parent) club. National clubs are a great source of information on your breed. You can get the name of the secretary of the club by contacting:

The American Kennel Club
51 Madison Avenue
New York, NY 10010
(212) 696-8200

There are also numerous all-breed, individual breed, obedience, hunting and other special-interest dog clubs across the country. The American Kennel Club can provide you with a geographical list of clubs to find ones in your area. Contact them at the above address.

Registry Organizations

Registry organizations register purebred dogs. The American Kennel Club is the oldest and largest in this country, and currently recognizes over 130 breeds. The United Kennel Club registers some breeds the AKC doesn't (including the American Pit Bull Terrier and the Miniature Fox Terrier) as well as many of the same breeds. The others included here are for your reference; the AKC can provide you with a list of foreign registries.

American Kennel Club
51 Madison Avenue
New York, NY 10010

United Kennel Club (UKC)
100 E. Kilgore Road
Kalamazoo, MI 49001-5598

American Dog Breeders Assn.
P.O. Box 1771
Salt Lake City, UT 84110
(Registers American Pit Bull Terriers)

Canadian Kennel Club
89 Skyway Avenue
Etobicoke, Ontario
Canada M9W 6R4

National Stock Dog Registry
P.O. Box 402
Butler, IN 46721
(Registers working stock dogs)

Orthopedic Foundation for Animals (OFA)
2300 E. Nifong Blvd.
Columbia, MO 65201-3856
(Hip registry)

Activity Clubs

Write to these organizations for information on the activities they sponsor.

American Kennel Club
51 Madison Avenue
New York, NY 10010
(Conformation Shows, Obedience Trials, Field Trials and Hunting Tests, Agility, Canine Good

Citizen, Lure Coursing, Herding, Tracking,
Earthdog Tests, Coonhunting.)

United Kennel Club
100 E. Kilgore Road
Kalamazoo, MI 49001-5598
(Conformation Shows, Obedience Trials, Agility,
Hunting for Various Breeds, Terrier Trials and
more.)

North American Flyball Assn.
1342 Jeff St.
Ypsilanti, MI 48198

International Sled Dog Racing Assn.
P.O. Box 446
Norman, ID 83848-0446

North American Working Dog Assn., Inc.
Southeast Kreisgruppe
P.O. Box 833
Brunswick, GA 31521

Trainers

Association of Pet Dog Trainers
P.O. Box 3734
Salinas, CA 93912
(408) 663–9257

American Dog Trainers' Network
161 West 4th St.
New York, NY 10014
(212) 727–7257

**National Association of Dog Obedience
Instructors**
2286 East Steel Rd.
St. Johns, MI 48879

Associations

American Dog Owners Assn.
1654 Columbia Tpk.
Castleton, NY 12033
(Combats anti-dog legislation)

Delta Society
P.O. Box 1080
Renton, WA 98057-1080
(Promotes the human/animal bond through
pet-assisted therapy and other programs)

Dog Writers Assn. of America (DWAA)
Sally Cooper, Secy.
222 Woodchuck Ln.
Harwinton, CT 06791

National Assn. for Search and Rescue (NASAR)
P.O. Box 3709
Fairfax, VA 22038

Therapy Dogs International
1536 Morris Place
Hillside, NJ 07205